The
UNIVERSITIES
and the PUBLIC

The
UNIVERSITIES
and the PUBLIC

David N. Portman

A History of Higher
Adult Education
in the United States

Nelson-Hall *nh* Chicago

Library of Congress Cataloging in Publication Data

Portman, David N.
   The universities and the public.

   Bibliography: p.
   Includes index.
   1.   Adult education—United States—History.
   2.   Community and college—United States—History.
   I.   Title.
   LC5251.P6   374.9′73   78–9333
   ISBN 0–88229–116–5

Copyright © 1978 by David N. Portman

Manufactured in the United States of America

10   9   8   7   6   5   4   3   2   1

To my wife
and sons

Contents

	Preface	ix
	Introduction	xi
1.	American Education in a Century of Change	1
2.	Early Development of Adult Education	13
3.	Higher Education Reaches Out: The Experimental Years	37
4.	The Wisconsin Idea	79
5.	Years of Growth and Crisis	107
6.	The Modern Era	139
	Notes	175
	Bibliography	195
	Index	207

Preface

The subject of higher adult education has long been neglected by students of the American college and university. Although university extension is as old as the American university itself, the development of adult educational efforts has not been adequately reported by educational historians.

In my attempt to fill that void, I am greatly indebted to Lee Porter, dean of continuing education at Roosevelt University; David Dresser, vice-president of Eisenhower College; and Professors Nelson Blake, Sarah Short, Kline Hable, Harlan Copeland, and Robert Bickel of Syracuse University. Their comments were valuable in the development of this study, although responsibility for its accuracy is entirely my own.

I am particularly grateful to my wife and sons who, for many months, made special sacrifices in order that I might complete this project. Finally, I will always be indebted to my parents who, by voice and behavior, exemplified and fostered the inquiring mind in their children.

Introduction

Higher adult education, the extension of college and university resources to a wider public, has now completed approximately one hundred years of development in America. The purpose of this study is to examine the movement, the cultural conditions which made it possible, the persons who played key roles, the characteristics which distinguished each period, and the trends which emerged and continue to the present day.

A host of scholars and practitioners have written on higher adult education in one form or another for many years. Articles in educational and popular literary journals appeared as early as the 1880s. Since then, there has been a more or less continuous flow of studies and reports regarding university adult activity. During the late 1880s and early 1890s hundreds of essays and documents appeared as a result of English extension, Chautauqua activity, and initial university extension experiments in America. After this initial burst of energy, activity languished for a decade, and literature on the subject reflected that decline. No longer was extension the lively topic of discussion among educators that it had been in 1890.

Statewide commitment to higher adult education by the extension division of the University of Wisconsin in 1907 sparked a new wave of enthusiasm and, as an immediate result, extension shortly thereafter became a national phenomenon. The founding of the National University Extension Association in 1915 (as well as the founding of the Association of University Evening Colleges in 1939) evidenced that fact.

This study draws heavily from various journal articles and conference reports of organizations concerned with the promotion and administration of higher adult education. This material reflects, perhaps better than any other, the problems and issues which confronted the movement. Other interpretative sources (for example, Grattan's *In Quest of Knowledge,* Knowles' *The Adult Education Movement in the United States,* and Dyer's *Ivory Towers in the Market Place*) are used primarily as guideposts and points of departure. (No previous full-length study has been devoted exclusively to the first one hundred years of higher adult education in America.) In addition this work utilizes selected reports and statistics issued by the Office of Education. Caution should be taken in the interpretation of such materials, however, because for many years the data used were given voluntarily and reported to be incomplete.

This discussion of higher adult education is essentially limited to activity undertaken by the colleges and universities themselves. Particularly during the modern period, a case could be made for higher adult education promoted by noncollegiate institutions (public television, for example). Except as background, however, this activity is not reported.

Chapters 1 and 2 provide background information: the first deals with cultural and educational progress during the nineteenth century, and the second traces the noncollegiate roots of adult education. Chapters 3 through 6 are devoted to higher adult education proper as it evolved in America.

The intention of this study is to concentrate on the unique aspects of each period. For example, although evening and community colleges are still vigorous institutions for higher adult education, they are only discussed at length between the world wars (chapter 5), the period in which they emerged on the national scene.

This study does not attempt to be a statistical almanac from which numerical comparisons may be culled. Facts and figures are used only when they illustrate and support my central concerns: the character and expansion of the higher adult education movement in America.

For purposes of this study, "higher adult education" refers to general extension, evening college activity, and other community services undertaken by or associated with institutions of higher learning in the United States. The term includes programs sponsored by two- and four-year colleges as well as universities.

1

American Education
in a Century of Change

During the early decades of the nineteenth century the American people were chiefly concerned with the acquisition and cultivation of land. Having crossed the Appalachian mountains during the colonial and revolutionary periods, settlers spread throughout the eastern Mississippi Valley. Farm families grew rapidly on the productive land and the region was soon filled. With the prospect of cheaper land, easterners and offspring of pioneers continued the westward thrust throughout the nineteenth century.

While the population pushed westward to cover the land, not all settlement was rural. As the years passed, cities grew both in number and in size. Established early as supply and trading centers for the steadily increasing agricultural population, villages took on characteristics of self-sustaining entities, relying more on newly developing industries than on the farm market.

Paralleling the growth of the industrialized city was the rapidly developing system of railway transportation. Playing a vital role in the transition of the nation from an agricultural to an industrial economy, railroads hauled raw materials to factories and factory products to consumers. Foreign capital was attracted by railroad securities, while railroad promoters drew immigrants to the United States by advertising cheap land and high wages. Railroad profits provided capital for manufacturing plants, and railroads became the best customers for the iron and steel industries. Further, railroads made business national by opening new marketing territories and by forcing manufacturers all over the country to compete with one another.[1]

The immigration of other people, particularly Europeans, was a factor deeply involved in the transition of America from rural to urban orientation. Immigration played a minor role down to the 1840s in the settlement of western lands, the primary impact of the newly arriving population being in the formation of the cities. The first immigrants to affect the development of the cities were the Irish who settled in the major ports of the Northeast during the 1830s and 1840s. A second wave of millions of immigrants was to have an even more pronounced effect on the growth and character of the city: "In the early 1880s came a greater wave of the new immigrants—new in the double sense that they were no longer from western and northern Europe but from eastern and southern Europe, and that they were more likely to settle in the big cities and work in the mines and mills and factories than on the land."[2]

During the nineteenth century, the common man moved to gain control over his political institutions. Marking the shift from aristocratic leadership to popular leadership, Jacksonian Democracy ushered in an era of social reform which would continue into the twentieth century. This movement would be accompanied by an increasing spirit of self-improvement in American life. By the 1880s, Horatio Alger novels read by millions of boys would be promoting success and happiness through honest toil, faith, and education.

The momentous transition could not have taken place without shaking the foundations of the old order and necessitating profound economic and social readjustment. Never before had American society suffered from such a severe attack of growing pains. In this short period of time after the Civil War the nation was beset with industrial monopoly, political corruption, labor exploitation, and agrarian discontent.[3]

The complications of the period did not go unrecognized. Whereas the literate public earlier in the century had been offered the tales of Washington Irving and James Fenimore Cooper, by the 1890s novelists were increasingly turning their attention to less romantic matters. William Dean Howells, in *A Hazard of New Fortunes* (1889), dealt with the trials of middle-class urban people, emphasizing the dangers of newly acquired wealth. The isolation and despair of rural life were reported by Hamlin Garland in *Main-Travelled Roads* (1891). In *Maggie, A Girl of the Streets* (1892), Stephen Crane vividly portrayed the demoralizing influence of the city.[4]

The first century of the American nation, then, was one of remarkable and often painful growth. As part of the framework of this developing nation, institutions emerged which were expected to educate the growing population.

Public Education

While profound changes were affecting the way the American family supported itself and the environment in which it chose to live, the educational institutions which followed were also experiencing an evolution. Morison and Commager, commenting on nineteenth century educational conditions, concluded:

> The most tangible social gain during this period of ferment was in popular education. Since the Revolution education had been left largely to private initiative and benevolence. Secondary academies and colleges had been founded, and of those the South now had more than the North. But almost all these institutions charged fees. Elementary education . . . was then the most neglected branch. Most of the Northern states had some sort of public primary system, but only in New England was it free and open to all. In some instances a child had to be taught his letters before he was admitted to one of these schools, and in others only those pleading poverty were exempted from fees. In addition the Quakers and other philanthropic bodies maintained charity schools for the poor. Consequently a stigma was attached to the free schools. In New York City, around 1820, nearly half the children went uneducated because their parents were too poor to pay fees, and too proud to accept charity.[5]

While Massachusetts led the nation in public education, as late as 1837, one-third of the state's children received no schooling at all. Of those fortunate enough to attend school, many did so for only two months out of the year.[6] In 1852, under the leadership of Horace Mann, Massachusetts passed a compulsory attendance law which required every child to attend school for a certain period of years. Despite opposition from private schools and those who objected to the required taxes, other states soon followed Massachusetts.

Initially the wealthy classes opposed public education. In time, however, some upper-class leaders came around to the position that an educated working class was the best insurance against revolution: An ignorant populace might attack private property. Public school teachers could take care of that by teaching youngsters to cherish established institutions and respect authority."[7] Reformers believed the public schools would reduce the distinctions among the classes, remove children from industrial employment, and generally allow young people of all classes to improve themselves socially and economically.

But while New York City in 1832 and Philadelphia in 1836 established public elementary schools free from the taint of charity, the growth of public schools did not keep pace with the increase in population by birth and immigration. There were approximately half a million white adult illiterates in the country in 1840 and almost one million by 1859.[8] In the South, similar conditions prevailed with the Negro being prohibited from learning to read in many states.

On the heels of the developing primary school, a second revolution was unfolding: "The greater part of this revolution . . . occurred since the closing decades of the nineteenth century, when it [the academy] was transformed into a higher common school whose chief task [was] not the preparation of young people for college studies but the preparation of young people for the real business of living."[9]

Little doubt the rise of the public high school, in part, made possible the democratic trends which characterize higher education between the Civil War and the end of the century. As more and more attended public schools beyond the primary grades, the gap between the majority of people and higher learning became less marked. By the 1890s substantial numbers of Americans had achieved at least some education beyond the secondary level from contact with colleges and universities.

Nineteenth Century Colleges and Universities

The early American college owed its expansion largely to the support of various religious denominations. While only a few colleges had been established during the colonial period, a substantial increase in the total number of institutions took place during the nineteenth century. Denominational competition greatly contributed to the proliferation of colleges which, as described by Tewksbury, were designed primarily to be "nurseries for ministers."[10] Reassured by the Dartmouth College decision, which held that a college charter was a contract which could not be impaired, bands of eastern missionaries carried their culture with messianic zeal to Ohio, Indiana, Illinois, and other states of the old Northwest Territory.

Methodists, Presbyterians, and Congregationalists led in establishing colleges. Finally these efforts were so diffuse and demands for support so confusing that the Society for the Promotion of Collegiate and Theological Education at the West was organized in 1843 to coordinate the various denominational efforts.[11] Encouraged by the Yale Report of 1828, which defended the traditional classical subjects of Latin and Greek, the curriculum of the denominational colleges stabilized for half a century thereafter. Rejecting the more utilitarian modern languages and sciences, the colleges tended to attract students who were young in age and members of the upper social and economic stratum. In Tewksbury's frontier college there was little place for sons of the farm or urban worker.

Though the denominational college dominated higher education in America down to the Civil War, it did so in the face of growing opposition. Elitism, a chief characteristic of the old-time college, was in the end its major liability. From the revolutionary period onward, a small but growing band of critics called for reform along more democratic lines.

One aspect of that reform movement was the development of the state college and university. With the early thrust of the Jeffersonian ideal of training for democratic leadership and the Jacksonian legacy of mass education, state-supported higher education was not to be denied. Central to the rise of the state university was its curricular reformation along more practical lines. Higher instruction, said the industrial leaders, must be brought into harmony with the needs of a practical, growing people.

President Francis Wayland of Brown University told his trustees in 1850: "Lands were to be surveyed, roads to be constructed, ships to be built and navigated, soils of every kind, and under every variety of climate, were to be cultivated, manufactures were to be established which must soon come into competition with those of more advanced nations; and in a word, all the means which science has provided to aid the progress of civilization must be employed."[12] The classics and humanities should be supplemented by subjects helpful to industrial and agricultural progress, subjects that would lift the farmer and mechanic out of their old limitations. "What we want," Horace Greeley proclaimed, "are men with the expert skills to double our grain crops. . . ."[13]

During this same period of agricultural and industrial agitation for educational reform, pressure could be felt from adventurous scholars. Restricted by the narrow classical curriculum of the denominational college and with little opportunity for serious graduate work in the United States, determined students had, in increasing numbers, been forced to travel to Germany for specialization. Exposed to the German scientific approach to both the natural and social disciplines, these students returning to America soon achieved prominence and were among the most vocal in calling for reform of the college curriculum. The tradition of the American scholar studying in Germany began early in the nineteenth century, and by the 1850s considerable interest had developed concerning continental universities, which at that time were preeminent in the world.

In 1852 Henry Tappan assumed the presidency of the University of Michigan and declared that German institutions could serve as models for the new American university.[14]

While Tappan sought to make the University of Michigan the intellectual center of the state, he dismissed as artificial the distinction between intellectual and practical pursuits of the university: "We shall have no more acute distinctions drawn between scholastic and practical education; for, it will be seen that all true education is practical, and that practice without education is of little worth; and then there will be dignity, grace, and a restless charm about scholarship and the scholar."[15] Premature in his leadership and abrasive in his style, Tappan offended the Michigan trustees as well as the popular press and was dismissed in 1863.

Significant though the experiment at Michigan was, the rapid development of publicly supported colleges and universities during the latter half of the nineteenth century came primarily as a result of two legislative acts of the federal government. After years of political maneuvering and a presidential veto, in 1862 the first Morrill land-grant act was passed. This act, which did not receive popular attention at the time, was to play a major role in the reforming of American higher education. It provided for the support in every state of at least one college "where the leading object shall be, without excluding other scientific or classical studies, to teach such branches of learning as are related to agriculture and the mechanic arts."[16]

Thirty thousand acres of federal land for each senator and representative were given to each state. The states were then permitted to dispose of the lands, which consisted of some seventeen million acres in all, and use the resulting funds for support of the institutions. The statute permitted 10 percent of the funds to be used for the purchase of a college site or experimental farm land, the balance being

restricted for use as a continuing endowment. In the beginning, a great deal of confusion existed in many states as to
how the grant would be put to use. Each state had the right
to select the location and decide upon the character of the
colleges with certain limitations.

Existing colleges, suffering from declining revenues and
rising costs, discovered their eligibility to serve as land-
grant institutions and joined the competition. The state universities and private sectarian schools alike held out their
hands for federal grants. In some states (Michigan, Maryland, and Pennsylvania) existing state schools of agriculture were awarded benefits. An industrial university was
established in Illinois and a college of agriculture and mechanical arts appeared in Ohio. These two schools were
soon, however, transformed into state universities.[17]

In fifteen states, where the state university had become
well developed, the land-grant institution became a part of
the existing unit. In twenty-eight others it was established
as a separate agricultural and mechanical college (A & M).
In several states, private institutions accepted the grant,
although a number of grants were later withdrawn from a
few of these private schools. All too frequently the sale of
the public land was a dismal affair. Beyond the reckless
manner in which land was occasionally sold, the resulting
endowment investment was, at times, mismanaged. The
figures show a great disparity among states in actual resources realized, ultimately, by the land grant.

Cornell University conspicuously stood out for its shrewd
handling of federal lands. The Cornell property was selected and managed by Ezra Cornell, a skillful businessman
who had made a fortune with the Western Union Tele-
graph. The university lands, under Cornell's direction,
realized an average of just over $5.50 an acre on its million
acres, far greater than the national average price.[18]

After a number of years it became clear that the first

land-grant funding, in many instances, was inadequate. Justin Morrill, the Vermont legislator who had engineered the original act through Congress, continued to push for an expanded program of federal support for the colleges. After nearly twenty years of almost annual debate, Congress passed the second Morrill bill in 1890. This act provided for an initial appropriation of $15,000 for each land-grant college. The appropriation was then to be increased yearly by $1,000 to a maximum of $25,000 by the end of the century.[19]

In 1899 the United States Commissioner of Education reported sixty-four institutions supported by land-grant funds, fourteen of which were organized for Negroes in the South. These colleges enrolled over thirty-five thousand students pursuing programs in agriculture, mechanical engineering, civil engineering, electrical engineering, architecture, household economy, veterinary science, and military tactics. Endowment funds ranged from what amounted to negligible amounts for a number of colleges to over $6 million at Cornell University.[20]

Preceding the land-grant revolution but related to it, another type of post-secondary institution developed, the technical institute. Discounting the United States Military Academy at West Point, founded in 1802, the first of these special purpose schools, Rensselaer Polytechnic Institute at Troy, New York, was organized in 1824. Its purpose was the preparation of teachers "who would instruct sons and daughters of local farmers and mechanics in the art of applying science to husbandry, manufactures, and domestic economy."[21] In 1849 Rensselaer broadened its curriculum to include the study of architecture and civil, mining, and topographical engineering.

These new curricular changes were not entirely lost on the older liberal arts colleges. A number of colleges incorporated, in one way or another, engineering and technology

into their undergraduate programs. Under the direction of
Eliphalet Nott, the inventor-president of Union College in
Schenectady, New York, that school established a department of civil engineering in 1845. Shortly thereafter, Harvard founded its Lawrence Scientific School. Within a few
more years, Yale, Dartmouth, Brown, and the University
of Pennsylvania had created either scientific schools or departments of practical science.[22] Thereafter, the technical
institute developed in every section of the country. By
1897, forty-three schools of technology, many of which had
grown with land-grant support, enrolled over ten thousand
students.[23]

The impact of the broadened curriculum became particularly visible during the last thirty years of the nineteenth
century in the growth of graduate education. While the old-
time college, on occasion, conferred the master's degree,
it was generally a result of a year or two of resident teaching and study with the stress being on the teaching.

The first major attempt to transplant the German variety
of scholarship to this country was made by the Johns Hopkins University in Baltimore, Maryland. Johns Hopkins was
originally designed as a graduate institution with specialized
research training as its primary objective, although for
feeder purposes it did accommodate undergraduates. Its
first president, Daniel Coit Gilman, who had participated
in the reorganization of Yale's Sheffield Scientific School
after the Civil War, and many of the early faculty members,
had been trained in continental schools, both in England
and in Germany.[24]

While the Hopkins model of the independent, graduate
unit was not widely emulated, its impact on other institutions was, nonetheless, great. The forces which were to create the great Baltimore university were working on the
liberal arts colleges and, slowly, after the Civil War, Harvard, Yale, and Columbia expanded their graduate offer-

ings. In an address given on the twenty-fifth anniversary of the founding of Johns Hopkins, Harvard President Charles W. Eliot acknowledged the degree to which Hopkins had influenced higher education in America: "I want to testify that the Graduate School of Harvard University, started feebly in 1870 and 1871, did not thrive until the example of Johns Hopkins forced our faculty to put their strength into the development of our instruction for graduates. And what was true of Harvard University was true of every other university in the land which aspired to create an advanced school of the arts and sciences."[25]

By the end of the century, then, fairly clear lines of the modern American society had been drawn. The democratic impulse, which led to political reforms and during the progressive era would lend strength to economic reform, early influenced the development of education in America. Primary and secondary schools were firmly established, and while no grand commitment had been made, higher education had undergone great change and was no longer the exclusive property of the upper classes.

With the traditional form of higher education rapidly changing, it will be shown that by the 1880s colleges and universities entered a period of experimentation in which they sought to offer their resources to a broad adult population. Paralleling the growth of higher education that led to university experimentation, however, adult educational activity apart from the universities could also be observed. These early efforts in adult education will be discussed in the next chapter.

2

Early Development of Adult Education

As the historian C. Hartley Grattan has pointed out, American democracy rests on the assumption that man is educable, that it is possible to deliberately improve and sophisticate his ability to make rational decisions in all areas of life. For many years arguments in education have revolved around how to educate and what should be taught, not whether the people ought to be educated.[1] In the early years the American adult obtained knowledge primarily from informal sources, at his own pace, and according to his interest.

Newspapers, Magazines, and Libraries

Newspapers published during the eighteenth century were perhaps the first regular source of information available to the colonial population. The first newspaper, the

Newsletter, was produced in Boston in 1704.[2] In 1721 James Franklin, with the aid of his young brother Ben, published the *New England Courant.* By 1725, five newspapers existed in the colonies. Thereafter there was a rather rapid increase, and by 1765 there were twenty-five being published in the American colonies, two of them in German. Every colony except Delaware and New Jersey could boast a newspaper. Those early papers contrast sharply with their modern counterpart. They were all published weekly and ran four pages in length. In content they closely resembled the London papers, utilizing English clippings and augmenting these with a modest amount of local information, including death notices, laws, advertisements of runaway slaves, notices of mutiny, and the like.[3]

After the Revolution the newspaper continued to develop and traveled west with the population, stimulated by the growth of trade. In time, every self-respecting village could point with pride to its local paper. Unlike the colonial paper, the nineteenth century product became a rather substantial news-gathering operation, reporting regional and national news as well as local activity. Aided by advertising income and technological improvement, the *New York Sun,* the *New York Herald,* and others could market their papers at a price large numbers of people could afford. While precise figures are, of course, impossible to obtain, it seems safe to estimate that millions of adults during the eighteenth and nineteenth centuries did most of their reading from the Bible and the local newspaper.

Like the newspaper, the popular literary magazine came to enjoy wide distribution in America, particularly during the latter half of the nineteenth century. Magazines tended to develop along special interest as well as class lines. One of the early successful examples of high quality journalism was the *North American Review,* which had been established in 1815.[4] Journals aimed at farmers, mechanics, housewives, preachers, teachers, intellectuals, and ethnic groups rapidly reached the popular market. The advances in literacy, accompanied by technological improvements, resulted in the mass production of journals and, by 1895, the editor of *Munsey's* could boast of the first ten-cent magazine.[5]

After the Civil War many journals became somewhat more comprehensive in their content. It was not uncommon for a leading periodical, *Century,* for example, to include material on politics, biography, education, sports, antiquity, and fiction in a single issue. At the close of the Civil War some seven hundred magazines were published in the United States. By 1885, aided by the second-class postal privilege, the figure had jumped to 3,300.[6] Clearly, then, reading as a popular activity had become widespread in America.

The library originally developed in the colonies on a subscription basis. The earliest on record is the Library Company, organized by Benjamin Franklin in 1731. As an outgrowth of his discussion group, the Junto, this library was formed for the cooperative use of Junto members and other interested Philadelphians.[7] Subscription libraries and athenaeums became the basis for library development until the early nineteenth century when it began to weaken. For a time, mechanics' institutes and lyceum groups dominated library development with their modest collections. Of greatest importance, however, was the rise of another species, the publicly supported library, a phenomenon which occurred between 1800 and the 1830s. The Library of Congress, destroyed in the burning of the Capitol during the War of 1812, was established in the year 1800. State libraries were organized in New Hampshire, New Jersey, and Pennsylvania and eventually in each of the other states. Early school libraries also began to appear during this period. During the 1850s, states began to pass laws enabling towns to create public libraries, but many counties had already created libraries without the special legal authorization. The city of Boston was a leader in the public library movement, its promoters seeing the library as an extension of the public schools.[8]

The public library movement's chief driving force, however, came not from public demand but from the generosity of the steel magnate, Andrew Carnegie.[9] Eventually giving some $45 million in support of library construction, Carnegie made his first grant to the city of Pittsburgh in 1881. Under the Carnegie plan, the community furnished the site and Carnegie built the library which the community was then responsible to maintain.[10] In this way the local library was permanently welded to public support, and a vital phase of democratic education had been achieved.

The Lyceum

During the 1820s, before books and magazines were widely available, the popular thirst for knowledge led to the development of the lyceum. In 1826, there appeared in the *American Journal of Education* an outline of the plan, attributed to, though not signed by, one Josiah Holbrook:

> I take the liberty to submit for your consideration a few articles as regulations for associations for mutual instruction in the sciences, and in useful knowledge generally. . . . It seems to me that if associations . . . could be once started in our villages, and upon a general plan, they would increase with great rapidity, and do more for the general diffusion of knowledge and for raising the moral and intellectual taste of our coutrymen than any other expedient which can possibly be devised. And it may be questioned if there is any other way to check the progress of that monster, intemperance, which is making such havoc with talents, morals, and everything that raises man above the brute, but by present-

ing some object of sufficient interest to divert the attention
of the young from places and practices which lead to dissi-
pation and ruin.[11]

Holbrook proposed to raise man above the brute through
regular courses of instruction by lecture, but he did not rule
out the use of other methods including demonstration and
discussion. He further called for the creation of a hierarchy
of lyceums. He began with the local society for mutual instruction by proposing that it elect several delegates, who
were to represent the local to the county lyceum. Each
county board of lyceums then would appoint one of its
members to sit on the State Board of Mutual Education.
Not a man of limited objectives, Holbrook finally proposed
a General Board of Education embracing the United
States.[12]

Such a scheme must surely have seemed outlandish to
many who read it in the 1820s. Yet a large part of Holbrook's plan was actually put into effect. The Millbury
Branch Number 1 of the American Lyceum was the first
established. Within one year, ten neighboring villages had
their own lyceums, and in 1827 the Worcester County
Lyceum was organized. Traveling throughout New England
and promoting his cause, Holbrook stimulated, by 1828,
approximately one hundred communities to create lyceums.
Shortly thereafter, they spread to other sections of the
country, and by 1834 some three thousand town lyceums
existed as far west as Detroit and as far south as Florida.[13]

In 1831, delegates from one thousand locals met in New
York City to organize the National American Lyceum
whose specific goals were to be "the advancement of education, especially in the common schools, and the general diffusion of knowledge."[14] The National Lyceum lasted only
until 1839, its annual meetings being rather poorly attended
and its work largely accomplished. It has been credited
with having been a major force in the establishment of

public schools and the coordination of education at state and national levels.[15]

While the National Lyceum ran its course early, the local lyceum remained a strong cultural force in the community for many years. Some, but not all, of the lyceums were substantial operations capable of attracting (which meant paying) many of the more notable men of the day. Among the regular participants were such prominent citizens as Ralph Waldo Emerson, Henry David Thoreau, James Russell Lowell, Oliver Wendell Holmes, Louis Agassiz, Henry Ward Beecher, Horace Greeley, and Charles A. Dana.[16]

After the interrupton of the Civil War, the nature of the lyceum changed markedly. The movement took on a strong commercial cast with a variety of agencies first competing, then acting collectively, in the booking of star courses. As the years went by, the lyceum lecture became less serious in tone and took on the characteristics of simple entertainment.[17] Though the town lyceum had begun to fade by the Civil War, the reasons for its popularity lived on, and during the 1870s and 1880s, the Chautauqua Institution took up the torch of community improvement that the local lyceum had lit.

Vocational Institutes: Mechanics', Farmers', and Teachers'

Vocational education in a variety of special areas was offered to adults during much of the nineteenth century and often took the form of the institute. The mechanics' institute was originally developed in England between 1800 and 1825 under the direction of Dr. George Birkbeck, a professor of natural philosophy. These institutes attempted to teach workers the scientific principles behind their vocational practices. They taught such subjects as optics, mathematics, chemistry, heat, steam, hydraulics, and astronomy.

These institutes for mechanics spread rapidly not only over the British Isles, but to Canada, Australia, India, and the United States as well. While the stated purpose varied somewhat in each locale, the three fundamental propositions were that they should promote a knowledge of general science, diffuse rational information to the workers, and elevate character by providing worthwhile "intellectual pleasures" and "refined amusement."[18]

The American version was actually far more elaborate than the institution which had developed in England. The central features of the American institute were the library, lecture, and vocational training. In some cases, a local mechanics' institute would work in conjunction with or beside the local lyceum in its activities, particularly with regard to the libraries and lectures.[19]

The first mechanics' libraries were established by the (New York) Mercantile Library Association and the Apprentices' Library Association about 1820. These libraries were duplicated in many other communities and served as important sources of information for special groups until the public library entered the picture later in the century. In some cases the public library absorbed the collections held by the mechanics' associations.[20]

The special attention given to agricultural education developed somewhat later than education for the mechanic. While a few agricultural societies existed earlier, no substantial body of scientific information was available for dissemination until after the Civil War. Stimulated by the Morrill Act of 1862 and the Hatch Act of 1887, many farmers, by the end of the century, were receiving instruction offered by colleges through a variety of short courses or institutes, as well as literature from newly established experimental stations.

In 1863, Massachusetts organized one of the first farmers' institutes which then spread to many other states. The institutes ranged anywhere from two to five days in duration.

Lectures typically were offered in the morning and afternoon, with the evening hours taken up in popular entertainment.[21] The Kansas State Agricultural College professed in 1885 not only to give a "thorough industrial training to those students who seek it, but it also disseminates scientific truths of practical value to the people by means of a weekly paper, and holds a series of six farmers' institutes in different counties each winter. In these, various subjects of interest and importance to the farmers are discussed and efforts made to promote the welfare of the agricultural population in every way possible."[22] The farmers' institutes remained popular until World War I.

A third area of vocational education arose out of the public school movement. For many years, school teachers had little or no training for their profession. By the 1830s and 1840s, various organizations including the National Lyceum, as noted earlier, were calling for some form of systematic education for teachers in the common schools. In response to this, the teachers' institute, or short-term course, was offered, the first being formed by Henry Barnard in Hartford, Connecticut, in 1839, the same year Horace Mann opened the first normal school in Lexington, Massachusetts. By 1845 institutes were held in more than half the counties in New York State as well as in Ohio, Pennsylvania, New Hampshire, Rhode Island, and Massachusetts. By 1850 it was reported that thirty-nine counties in New York State gave instruction through institutes to more than a thousand teachers.[23]

The length of the institutes varied greatly, but generally they ran from one week to two months. The purpose of the institute was to learn the "art or practical technique" and the "science" or theory of teaching, with the emphasis being on the art.[24] The teachers' institutes were, in some instances, forerunners of normal institutes, and in most states they were absorbed by the normal schools. This conference type of training proved a popular activity and continues into the modern era, although teachers' colleges have declined.

The mechanics', farmers', and teachers' institutes were national movements which, for a period of time, were the dominant adult educational activity for the special interest groups which they served. Other organizations developed during the nineteenth century whose efforts were limited to their own locale. The following examples were organizations of essentially local initiative and local impact.

Cultural Institutes: Lowell and Cooper

Taking note of the lyceum and its successful utilization of the lecture method, an organization developed in Boston in 1836 known as the Lowell Institute. This institute was endowed with a trust fund by John Lowell, Jr.[25] When Lowell drew his will, at the age of thirty-three, he provided the means to "establish a series of public lecture courses, consisting of eight or twelve lectures in sequence, composed for an adult audience by the foremost authorities."[26] Since a program of this sort would be expensive if lectures were to be given by speakers from abroad, his will stipulated that no money should be spent for construction: a rented auditorium would serve well for the purpose. To insure a popular reception, only prominent men would be invited to the platform. The subject matter to be discussed was left to the speaker with one limitation: Lowell concluded that each year one course should be devoted to the historical and internal evidences of Christianity. The balance of the program was to range widely through "philosophy, natural history, and the arts and sciences."[27]

The Lowell Institute developed during the same period and in the same vicinity that Holbrook organized his early town lyceum. But Lowell's free public lectures were to be far more comprehensive than those offered through the lyceum. The lecture as a series, with its conscious attempt at organization and continuity, was an important character- istic of the Lowell Institute. Whereas such speakers as Wendell Phillips and Russell Conwell delivered their popu- lar lecture thousands of times to different audiences, Lowell sought to attract speakers with original treatments of their selected topics.

When John Lowell, Jr., died in 1836, the capital fund established amounted to a quarter of a million dollars which, as terms of the endowment stipulated, yielded an annual budget of $16,000. This was not a small sum of working capital when it is remembered that full Harvard professors (among the best paid in the land) were earning approximately $1,200 a year.[28] The trusteeship of the in- stitute was placed in the hands of a brother, John Amory Lowell, who secured the Odeon and Tremont Theatres for the lectures.

On the evening of 3 January 1840 Governor Edward Everett officially opened the first course by introducing Professor Benjamin Silliman of Yale University (a promi- nent and durable figure in American education), who de- livered a series of twelve lectures on geology. With this promising start, sixty-four lectures were given during the first year of operation. Joining Silliman in the second sea- son was Sir Charles Lyell, a world-famous scientist, of whom Charles Darwin later remarked: "The science of geology is enormously indebted to Lyell—more so, I be- lieve, than any other man who ever lived."[29]

From the start the attendance at the free Lowell lectures was great; in some cases the demand for seats far exceeded the capacity of the auditorium. Following Silliman and Lyell in subsequent years were such notable figures as Louis Agassiz, Mark Hopkins, William Thackeray, Oliver

Wendell Holmes, Charles Eliot Norton, and William Dean Howells, to name only a few. With endowed financial backing, the Lowell Institute became a permanent educational fixture in the Boston area reaching, over the decades, millions of people.

During those early years, the center section of the first two rows, the pit as it was called, was roped off for members of the Lowell family and friends. The larger part of the audience, apparently, was made up of people from the working classes, particularly girls employed in the nearby textile mills. An early lecturer commented on his days at the "Lowell Lyceum" as he called it:

> During those palmy years of the Offering I used, every winter, to lecture for the Lowell Lyceum. Not amusement but instruction was then the Lyceum lecturer's sole aim, and however dry he or his subject might be, if he only conveyed knowledge which his hearers did not already possess he was listened to with profound attention. The Lowell Hall ... as we used to call it ... was always crowded, and four-fifths of the audience were factory girls. When the lecturer entered, almost every girl had a book in her hand, and was intent upon it. When he rose, the books were laid aside, and paper and pencil taken instead; and there were very few who did not carry home ... notes of what they had heard. I have never seen anywhere so assiduous note-taking—no, not even in a college class, when the notes might be of avail in an impending examination—as in that assembly of young women, laboring for their subsistence, many of whom in after life filled honorable, useful, and in some instances conspicuous positions in society.[30]

While the Lowell Institute proved successful over the years, perhaps owing to its unique backing, it was not so widely emulated as were the lyceums, vocational institutes, and, as we shall learn, the Chautauqua Institution. In at least one case, however, the Cooper Institute, the experience at Lowell was carefully considered from the beginning. The

Cooper Union, or Institute as it was originally known, was established in 1859 when Peter Cooper of New York deeded to six trustees, "All that . . . land bounded on the west by Fourth Avenue, and on the north by Astor Place, and on the east by Third Avenue, and on the south by Seventh Street, with all the furniture, rents and income . . . , to be forever devoted to the advancement of science and art in their application to the varied and useful purposes of life."[31]

Cooper had been impressed while in Paris with the type of teaching in schools of arts and trades, whose students were reputed to be living on a crust of bread in order to attend lectures:

> I recalled the time when there was no nightschool in New York or any means by which a poor boy could acquire knowledge except in the ordinary schools which required both time and money. I then formed a resolute determination that, if I could ever get the means, I would build an institution and throw its doors open at night as well as in the day, that the young people of this city might enjoy the advantages of knowledge, which would enable them to improve their condition and fit them for all the varied and useful purposes of life.[32]

Cooper had a special interest in the advancement of women, noting their difficult predicament in that urban environment:

> To manifest the deep interest and sympathy I feel in all that can advance happiness and better the condition of the female portion of the community, and especially of those who are dependent upon honest labor for support, I desire the trustees to appropriate two hundred and fifty dollars yearly to assist such pupils of the Female School of Design as shall in their careful judgement, by their efforts and sacrifices in the performance of duty to parents . . . make them

dependent on them for support, merit and require such aid.[33]

In addition to the deeded property, Cooper gave the trustees $10,000 in operating capital and for years continued to play an active role in the affairs of the institute. Upon his death, in the early 1880s, he willed an additional $100,000, and at his direction his children contributed a similar amount. In executing Cooper's mandate, the trustees of the institute laid down, as a basic principle, the intellectual improvement of the working class. Four areas of instruction were to be promoted: (1) branches of knowledge which were related to daily occupations, (2) instruction in personal hygiene and general family health, (3) instruction in the various social and political sciences, and (4) instruction in the creative arts, particularly as they related to recreation.[34]

The Cooper Institute, benefiting from the experience of the Lowell Institute, and with even greater resources, developed as a more comprehensive institution than Lowell in both style and substance. By the end of its first twenty-five years of operation, the institute embraced six departments:

(1) *A Free Reading Room and Library* housing some 400 periodicals and 17,000 books, which attracted over half a million visitors in 1883.

(2) *A Free Art School for Women* which accommodated some 275 persons of the 1,450 applicants.

(3) *A Free School for Women in Wood-Engraving* which attracted 32 students.

(4) *A Free School of Telegraphy for Women* which accepted 55 of the 160 applicants.

(5) *A Free Night School of Science* which offered a great variety of lectures taken by 1,169 students, most re-

maining until the close of the year, and about 400 of whom obtained certificates.

(6) *A Free Night School of Art* which included mechanical drawing, architecture, form drawing, free hand, and modeling, with an enrollment of 1,800 students.[35]

Like the Lowell Institute, the Cooper Institute, though modified over the years, had a significant impact on the community it served. Like Lowell, it attracted a segment of the community that most public schools and colleges ignored for the most part until the early years of the twentieth century. The Lowell and Cooper models were not widely copied, as they required a large concentration of people, as well as substantial philanthropic backing. During the middle nineteenth century these two limitations were significant. Nonetheless, a few other institutes did develop during this period, notably, the Goodwyn Institute of Memphis, Tennessee, the Drexel Institute of Philadelphia, and the Peabody Institute of Baltimore.[36]

Correspondence Study

Perhaps the most widely used medium of adult education in America before the Civil War was the lecture. But the lecture had its limitations, and within a few years after the Civil War another method of learning, correspondence study, was developing and offered promise of being somewhat more systematic than the lecture. Often as not, the lecture was treated as a one-shot affair with little or no coordination with previous or subsequent educational activity. Correspondence study on the other hand could provide regular and systematic learning to anyone so motivated and capable of doing the work, regardless of his geographical situation.

The earliest known correspondence study program took place in Germany in 1856, where a teacher of French in Berlin, Charles Toussant, in league with the writer Gustav Langenscheidt, formed a school for the teaching of languages by correspondence. Each student was sent a printed letter with drills in grammar and composition, supplemented with a continuing story in the language taught. The student was expected to forward a written recitation to the instructors who, in turn, criticized and returned it with comments.[37] Some years thereafter, correspondence study was incorporated into university extension work in England where its use became extensive.

In America, the first organized work involving correspondence study emerged during the 1870s. Anna Eliot Ticknor, the daughter of the prominent reform-minded Harvard professor, George Ticknor, founded the first correspondence instruction program in the United States in 1873. This Boston-based organization was known as the Society to Encourage Studies at Home. Regular monthly correspondence with directed readings and frequent examinations were the essential part of the society's instruction.[38] Like the Cooper and Lowell Institutes, the society hoped to reach the lower classes and working women in particular:

> Instead of confining our offers of help . . . to the wealthy class only, we at once endeavored to interest all classes, for we thought all needed us, though for different reasons, as all are liable to the consciousness of deficiency, general or special, in their education, and all may feel the need of encouragement to overcome some obstacle, it may be want of opportunity, or it may be the lack of energy to use the existing opportunities. Instead of mere plans for work without correspondence, and the irksome requirement of presence at headquarters at the end of each year, for competitive examinations and prizes, we adopted monthly correspondence,

> with frequent tests of results, desiring to produce intellectual
> habits and resources, without competition, and without ever
> fostering the desire to reach certain points at certain
> moments.[39]

Working with as many as two hundred helping volunteers, Miss Ticknor set about distributing books she had
collected, engravings, photographs, and any other tools
which might have facilitated the student's learning experience. The membership fee initially was two dollars yearly,
and later raised to three. After a period of time this permitted the operation to become self-supporting. Strangely,
she did not advertise in any of the popular publications
which might have reached interested students. "If it is
really needed," she remarked, "it will soon make itself
known."[40] The society reached a peak in 1882 enrolling
approximately one thousand students. Six departments or
areas of study were developed, History, Science, Art, Literature, French, and German, with a total of twenty-four
individual course offerings. Whether the aversion to publicity or dissatisfaction with the quality of instruction was
to blame, the organization declined in the 1890s and upon
Miss Ticknor's death in 1897 ended its activities.[41]

The value of the emerging correspondence study method
being duly noted, in 1883 a group of university professors
set about establishing the Correspondence University. This
was one of the earliest attempts by college and university
professors of several institutions to jointly sponsor instruction. There is, however, no evidence that the home institutions of the various participating professors joined in to
support the activity.

Little is known about the organization beyond attention
it was given by the press in 1883:

> A college professor has conducted by correspondence the
> mathematical studies of advanced pupils, and with such

satisfactory results that thirty-two professors in various colleges, from Harvard University in the East to the Johns Hopkins University in the South and the University of Wisconsin at the West, have united to form what is called for convenience the Correspondence University for the purpose of instruction by correspondence. The word university applies to the range of studies, which embraces a great number of branches, rather than to the organization, which is not chartered, and which has no authority to confer degrees. The scheme of education . . . is designed to supplement that of other institutions of education, and not to rival or oppose them. It is specifically intended to assist the following class of persons: those who are engaged in professional studies which can be taught by correspondence; graduates of colleges engaged in advanced studies; tutors and younger teachers in schools, academies and colleges; officers and men in the army and navy; young men and women employed in shops and upon farms who cannot leave their daily work to attend school or college; persons who propose to try the civil service examinations; and persons of any age and occupation who wish to pursue any particular study at home.[42]

The Correspondence University was, then, an organization of individuals, not institutions, although its base of operation was Cornell University. This attempt at teaching by mail did not thrive and no further mention is made of it in subsequent literature in either higher or adult education. It seems reasonable to assume that the Correspondence University suffered in the shadow of the rapidly emerging Chautauqua Institution, which will be discussed in detail later. By 1883 Chautauqua was already national in scope and receiving great acclaim from the press and enrolling thousands in its study program.

As early as 1873, an old denominational institution, Illinois Wesleyan University, was undertaking nonresident study under the leadership of Bishop Samuel Fallows. Not only did this school offer correspondence study, but after successfully passing examinations and writing a thesis, the student was granted a degree. Looking back on his thirty years at Illinois Wesleyan, Dean Graham commented:

> The grateful expressions from the many who have felt themselves benefited by the thorough and systematic work required and the words of approval from hosts of others, some of these among the leading educators, convince the faculty and board of the university that these courses meet and satisfy a wide demand for systematic home-study courses, with incentives in the way of proper academic recognition on successful completion.[43]

Under Bishop Fallows and Dean Graham the university did grant many correspondence degrees, both undergraduate and graduate, including the Ph.D. The university even published a magazine, directed to its correspondents, which was intended to keep them in touch with college life. Graham's effort on behalf of correspondence study went by the board, however. In the face of rising criticism from the academic community, which was increasingly concerned with standards (the North Central Association of Colleges and Universities was established about this time), nonresident instruction for undergraduates was dropped in 1903, and in 1906 all such instruction at Illinois Wesleyan was discontinued.[44]

The Illinois Wesleyan story is fairly well known to scholars of higher and adult education, its correspondence activity reappearing, from time to time, in the modern literature. Not so well documented in educational history, however, is the extent to which many other colleges and universities during the 1880s and 1890s were involved in nonresidential degree programs including the doctorate.

By the end of the academic year 1898–99, some forty-eight colleges and universities in the United States recognized by the Bureau of Education (at that time a division of the Department of Interior) were granting earned Ph.D.

degrees. In all, these institutions conferred the doctorate upon 325 students in 1899.[45] Most of these schools subscribed to such general requirements for doctoral study as: (1) a knowledge of French and German sufficient for purposes of investigation, which usually meant a reading knowledge, (2) an earned bachelor's degree from a reputable institution, (3) three years (in most cases) of advanced study and research, the last year of which was usually spent in residence at the degree-conferring institution, (4) the pursuit of one major subject and usually two minor subjects, (5) a thesis upon some approved subject which gave evidence of the candidate's ability to do original work, (6) and an examination in all subjects studied by the candidate.[46]

While the majority of schools surveyed by the Bureau of Education in 1898 generally conformed to the above practices, more than a few did not. "A number of institutions . . . conferring the Ph.D. degree," concluded the bureau, "do not provide instruction leading to that degree, but allow students to pursue the prescribed courses in absentia and to pass examinations at their homes under the supervision of a sentinel."[47]

Of the seventy-two institutions which supplied catalogs to the Bureau of Education, the following examples abstracted from the Report of the Commissioner of Education include those which relied most heavily on nonresident study.

Northern Illinois College, Fulton, Illinois

Nonresident graduate courses leading to the degree of doctor of philosophy are offered to persons who can furnish satisfactory evidence of having completed a regular college course or its equivalent in some approved institution of learning. Upon the successful completion of the course, a thesis upon some subject bearing upon some branch of the work and approved by the faculty, containing at least five thousand words, will be required, and upon proving satisfactory the degree will be duly granted. The examinations may be taken where the student resides or he may come to the college. If taken at home, the examination is taken in the presence of an examiner chosen by the student. The papers are examined at the college.

University of Wooster, Wooster, Ohio

The Ph.D. degree shall be conferred upon candidates having bachelor's degrees on the completion of a major course with a minor course in cognate studies. The major course consists of two parts, each of which represents an amount of work which, under favorable circumstances, may be accomplished in a year, and a minor course represents about one year's work. Residence at the university is not required, and examinations in absentia may be arranged whereby students may pass written examinations, other than final, under supervision approved by the faculty. The thesis required of candidates shall ordinarily contain from five to ten thousand words and is expected to be either a contribution to human knowledge, as embodying the results of original research, or such a discussion of a subject as by new and clearer exposition will lead to more ready acceptance and wider diffusion of established truth.

American Temperance University, Harriman, Tennessee

Students may enter any one of the graduate courses at any time and pursue their studies under the immediate direction of the faculty. Nonresident students may take the courses largely by correspondence. In special cases examinations in absentia may be arranged by the faculty. On the payment of required fees and the presentation of a thesis of three thousand words on an accepted theme the master's degree, corresponding to the bachelor's degree already received, will be conferred. At the end of the second year's work, in accordance with the same requirements, the Ph.D. degree will be conferred.[48]

The three examples cited above were not representative of all forty-eight institutions granting earned doctorates. In most cases, including all public institutions, the option for nonresident work meant credit to be accepted from another institution. A number of these schools, however, referred to nonresidential work as correspondence study. The growing question of academic standards and the abuse of what may have passed for correspondence "study" ended such activities for not only Illinois Wesleyan but many other private colleges and universities as well.

Most of these smaller denominational "universities" were actually four-year colleges which very frequently enrolled nearly as many high school or preparatory students as bachelor's degree candidates. Gale College, for example, which awarded fifteen doctorates in 1899, had at that time thirty-five preparatory school students, fifty undergraduates, and thirty graduate students.[49] Under these circumstances, it comes as no surprise that correspondence study encountered a great deal of resistance during the early years of the twentieth century.

Motivation for the private colleges to engage in correspondence study is not particularly hard to determine. However, throughout much of the nineteenth century, denominational colleges, particularly, were very hard pressed financially. Those colleges and universities offering correspondence study programs for degrees could not be considered prestigious institutions. They were marginal in a market of oversupply. As such, the application of strict standards for either residential or nonresidential work certainly would have diminished their prospects for survival. The possibility of additional income from nonresidential students must have been a great attraction to more than one beleaguered president who was continually hustling for cash, books, and buildings to keep his institution alive.

Another type of correspondence school developed totally apart from those mentioned above. During the 1880s, one Thomas J. Foster, the proprietor and editor of a daily newspaper published in the coal area of eastern Pennsylvania, became concerned with the dangers of coal mining as it was then practiced. At that time, coal mining was a major industry which experienced a great many worker deaths every year. Foster concluded that ignorance on the part of both owners and workmen was the chief culprit. He started his campaign for mine safety with a single column of questions and answers on mining practices in his paper. After a state law was passed requiring mine foremen to pass an examination on "safe methods and means of controlling dangerous natural phenomena incidental to coal mining," Foster stepped up his campaign by publishing several books on the prevention of mine disasters.[50]

Having aroused the public to the situation, Foster developed a course covering general practices in coal mining, surveying, and mine machinery in 1891. Receiving favorable response from both workers and superintendents, he extended his course. After inquiries came in from people with interests in allied fields such as engineering, drafting, and machinery, Foster created courses suited to their problems. So began the International Correspondence Schools of Scranton, Pennsylvania, as it was called, which over the years grew to be the largest and best-known profit-oriented correspondence school in the world. Ten years after the school opened, it was enrolling a quarter of a million students.[51] Foster demonstrated that correspondence study dealing with utilitarian subject matter could be a useful and successful method of learning.

The diversity which characterizes adult education today

was clearly evident, then, in the nineteenth century. Reading, the lecture, correspondence, and training in vocational skills were methods more or less commonly used. As diverse as the method, however, was the content of adult education which dealt with cultural, recreational, and vocational subject matter. In addition, the disparate nature of the institutions promoting adult education, the lyceums, the institutes, the colleges, and the press, added to this overall picture of uncoordinated activity. After the Civil War, however, there evolved a movement to systematize adult education, and the following chapters will reflect that development.

3

Higher Education Reaches Out: The Experimental Years

During the 1870s and 1880s educators were increasingly concerned with the problem of making the adult education process more systematic. Perhaps the first great effort in this direction was made by a remarkable educational network based in the southwest corner of New York State.

Chautauqua

The principal founder and guiding genius of Chautauqua was John Heyl Vincent. Vincent was described by his protégé, William Rainey Harper, as a man of calm and quiet, characterized by religious vigor, sturdy adherence to principle and high intellectual ideals, zealous for right living and religion.[1] At the age of nineteen Vincent became a minister of the Methodist church, without benefit of formal college education. His dedication to his profession, on the other hand, enhanced his desire for learning—a desire which he instilled in so many others during his lifetime. In 1866 he became interested in Sunday school work and particularly the problems of the Sunday school teacher. Some years later he founded the *Northwestern Sunday-School Quarterly* and developed the International Lesson System which had a great influence on the method of Bible study in the United States.[2]

After the Civil War, Vincent was transferred by his church to New York where he became the general agent of the Sunday School Union, an organization which directed Methodist-Episcopal Sunday schools throughout the world. While with the Sunday School Union he helped organize study-classes for teachers, and lectures given by these prominent instructors in major cities often drew a thousand or more. In the early 1870s, Vincent assumed the editorship of the *Sunday School Journal,* increasing its circulation from 5,000 to 200,000 within a few years. During the same period he set about establishing normal classes or weekly meetings of Sunday school teachers with definite courses of study, regular examinations, and diplomas for those who met its standards.[3]

With his normal class enjoying great popular success, Vincent conceived of a broader scheme for Sunday school teachers. His plan was to bring together "a large body of teacher-students, who should spend at least a fortnight in daily study, morning and afternoon, and thus accomplish more work than in six months of weekly meetings. He aimed also to have lectures on inspiring themes, with a spice of entertainment to impart variety."[4] This plan ultimately became the basis for the residential Chautauqua: the summer assembly.

While John Vincent was the chief intellectual and spiritual architect of the Chautauqua Institution, were it not for Lewis Miller of Akron, Ohio, all that has come to be associated with Chautauqua might never have been achieved. Miller was a mechanical genius with strong interests in both religious and popular education. Early in life he enjoyed success as a manufacturer of the Buckeye Mower, a device he invented which revolutionized the farm-machinery industry. His wealth brought him considerable prominence and, after being made president of the Mount Union College Board of Trustees in 1867, he was appointed by the Ohio governor to a state board for the purpose of devising a land-grant plan for a state school of mechanical and agricultural arts.[5]

Like Vincent, Miller had become active in promoting the normal class and due to Vincent's position in the Sunday School Union the two men met frequently after 1868. The friendship grew with the passing years and by 1873 the two made plans for the first Sunday School Assembly to be held in the summer of 1874 on the shores of Lake Chautauqua in the southwest corner of New York State. The site had for several years been used for summer camp meetings. Miller, as the official chairman, was to provide the financial backing for the operation and Vincent, head of the Department of Instruction, would direct its activities which in the early years emphasized, as would be expected, the training of Sunday school teachers.

Four years after the first summer assembly at Chautauqua the Chautauqua Literary and Scientific Circle was born. The CLSC was described by Vincent as a school at home, a school after school, a college for one's own house. The aim of the correspondence program was set forth in its many circulars:

> This organization aims to promote habits of reading and study in nature, art, science, and in secular and sacred literature, in connection with the routine of daily life (especially among those whose educational advantages have been limited), so as to secure to them the college student's gen-

eral outlook upon the world and life, and to develop the
habit of close, connected, persistent thinking. It encourages
individual study in lines and by textbooks which shall be indicated; by local circles for mutual help and encouragement
in such studies; by summer courses of lectures and "student's sessions" at Chautauqua; and by written reports and
examinations.[6]

Vincent envisioned the CLSC as a school for high school
and college graduates, for people who neither entered high
school nor college, for merchants, mechanics, apprentices,
mothers, farm boys, shop girls, and for people of wealth
and leisure who did not know what to do with their time.
The Chautauqua Circle was not the first plan of home reading in the United States. As has been pointed out, Anna
Ticknor had founded a few years earlier the Boston-based
Society to Encourage Studies at Home. Jesse Hurlbut, an
active Chautauquan and author of *The Story of Chautauqua,* pointed out that the circle in some respects was not
dissimilar from Miss Ticknor's organization.[7] Vincent was
further influenced by the apparent success of the English
home reading circles and the National Home Reading
Union during the 1870s.[8] When planning the circle in
1878, Hurlbut quotes Vincent as asking him, "How many
do you think can be depended on to carry on such a course
of study?" To which the skeptical Hurlbut replied, "Oh,
perhaps a hundred. People who want to read will find
books and those who don't care for reading will soon tire
of serious study." Springing from his chair and walking ner-
vously across the room, Vincent is said to have responded,
"I tell you, Mr. Hurlbut, the time will come when you see
a thousand readers in the CLSC."[9]

Vincent's estimate was not out of line when one con-
siders that the Ticknor organization that year had enrolled
824 students.[10] On a Chautauqua platform on the after-

noon of Saturday, 10 August 1878, Dr. Vincent made the first public announcement of the CLSC suggesting that the first book to be used would be *Green's Short History of the English People*. Interested readers were requested to sign a slip of paper and forward it to the platform. By the end of the afternoon nearly seven hundred eager persons had joined the new correspondence arm of Chautauqua.

The bookstore instantly disposed of the half dozen copies of Green it had on hand and an order for fifty more was telegraphed to Harper Brothers in New York. On the following morning another order of fifty was sent and this was followed by a request for an additional one hundred copies. Day after day the demand increased and, astounded by the activity, Harpers telegraphed Vincent asking "for particulars as to the reason why everybody at an almost unknown place called Chautauqua had gone wild in demand for this book."[11]

This story is recounted because it says a good deal about the enthusiasm which the leaders of the movement were able to generate. This enthusiasm characterized Chautauqua for many decades and, in part, accounts for the romantic myth of Chautauqua which emerged in later years. The myth of frivolity, of course, was a distortion of the rather serious evangelical nature of Chautauqua up to the turn of the century.

The CLSC was designed as a four-year course of home study and, in all, the first class of 1882 enrolled 8,400 persons. During that first year eleven books on such subjects as English history, Greek history and life, English literature, astronomy, psychology, and Bible history were assigned. The members were required to sign a statement that the books had been read and optional examination sheets, wisely entitled Outline Memoranda, were sent to readers. The scholar was encouraged to consult his books or any other sources to obtain answers to the questions, thereby eliminating the terror normally associated with examinations.[12]

In 1880 the *Chautauquan,* "a Monthly Magazine Devoted to the Promotion of True Culture and Organ of the Chautauqua Scientific and Literary Circle," made its first appearance. The journal was founded and edited by Dr. Theodore Flood, who successfully directed it for many years. The *Chautauquan* contained the list of required books for the year and included articles which students were requested to read. In addition the journal told readers how to organize local circles and lectures, and reprinted at great length correspondence and testimonials which flooded the organization's headquarters.[13] By 1886 the circulation of the *Chautauquan* reached 50,000 copies and was still growing and circled the globe. The magazine rivaled in circulation the best-known popular journals of the day.

From an initial enrollment of 8,400, by 1884 the enrollment for the entering class had jumped to over 20,000. During the middle 1880s it was said approximately 100,000 people in all were reading the *Chautauquan,* most of them enrolled CLSC students.[14] The class of 1885 graduated 1,250 readers from thirty-eight states. Well over 80 percent of those earning diplomas that year were women.[15]

Chautauqua attracted students from highly diverse backgrounds. Commented the editor of the *Chautauquan*:

> Thousands of members are college graduates and many have been sent into college by the stimulus of the work. There are hundreds of cultured homes represented in the membership. Lawyers, doctors, teachers, ministers and business men join the circle. But the great aim of the C.L.S.C. is to reach the poor, the uneducated, the neglected, the sick, and the old, and wonderfully well has it carried out its design. In many factory towns of New England and the Mid-

dle States are to be found circles of hard-working factory hands who steal time to read the prescribed course after ten hours of hard labor. On the plains of the west, in the mountains, far away from railroads and post-offices, readers are scattered. There are members in the Massachusetts Reformatory, and the penitentiaries at Canon City, Colorado, and Seattle, Washington Territory. . . . Many invalids throughout the country are making their shut-in hours bright . . . and among the aged [C.L.S.C.] work has been most successful. On Recognition Day last, were three deaf and dumb persons and one colored man, signs of the wide adaptability and endless opportunity which the course affords.[16]

The local circles of the CLSC were organized ostensibly to discuss readings of the month and hear lecturers, but there seems little doubt that their popularity was due, in part, to the social benefits of members meeting in each other's homes. The following report, one of thousands received at Chautauqua headquarters and published in the *Chautauquan,* was not atypical:

Our local circle of the C.L.S.C. in Bradford, Pennsylvania is one of several in this place, and is designated the Longfellow-Class in distinction from the others. We have limited our number to ten members, thinking by that means to promote individual interest. We have but two officers, a president and a secretary. We meet weekly, at the homes of different members. We have no leader appointed for the year, but every four weeks one member of the class is elected conductor of the exercises for the ensuing month. The manner of reviewing the lessons varies. The conductor sometimes asks questions, and, the topics are freely discussed by all; sometimes the subjects are apportioned to individual members to be talked over, or a synopsis of certain portions given by them. At the close of the lesson, fifteen minutes is devoted to discussing all rhetorical errors made during the evening.[17]

Over the years lectures became increasingly popular with

the local circles and were given most frequently by local school teachers and ministers. Occasionally a fortunate circle might entice a professor from a nearby college to expound upon his specialty, science and social issues especially being subjects warmly received by isolated Chautauquans.

Of those who registered at the beginning for a CLSC course, about one-quarter over the years reported at the end of four years that they had read the whole course. Many of the eager students read more than the required minimum number of books and articles. To those who finished the minimum collection of readings, a formal diploma was given, and, for those who read more, additional seals were stamped on the certificate.[18] It became a tradition to present the diploma at the various regional summer assemblies which sprang up around the country resembling the mother Chautauqua in New York State.

The CLSC was the most important but not the only division of the organization which utilized correspondence study. While the CLSC was described by Vincent as a correspondence program, more accurately it was a home-study plan, and though reader-teacher correspondence did take place, it was not a diploma requirement. During the 1880s specialized courses of reading and study were developed in five areas: history, literature, science, art, and pedagogy. Work in these areas earned the student a formal certificate. A School of Theology conducted courses of instruction through the mails and upon passage of "personally supervised rigid examinations" granted the B.D. degree.[19]

The College of Liberal Arts offered degrees of B.A. and B.S. for the successful completion of sixteen courses and supervised examinations. The work in the College of Liberal Arts was directed by professors while in residence at their home institutions. Degree programs were offered in the classics, humanities, social sciences, mathematics, modern languages, and the natural sciences.[20] The Chautauqua Institution was empowered by the regents of the University of the State of New York to grant not only the B.A. and B.S. of the College of Liberal Arts, but the M.A. and Ph.D. as well.[21]

Chautuaqua during those early days came to mean three more or less distinct adult educational activities. The correspondence work described above was perhaps the most important of the three. The second element which also received wide attention was the annual summer assembly at Chautauqua, New York. The duration and type of programs at summer Chautauqua varied from year to year.

The session of 1885 was divided into several overlapping sessions. In the July meetings, the Schools of Language and the Teacher's Retreat met for a period of three weeks. One hundred sixty persons attended the Schools of Languages representing twenty-three states. The Teacher's Retreat was directed by Professor J. W. Dickinson and it was reported that two-thirds of those participating in the program were experienced teachers. The instruction was intended to be of a practical nature: "The teachers, after having been instructed to develop minds instead of erecting machines in their pupils, were not left without methods for doing this. . . . Professors Martin and Kendall gave admirable illustrations for logical teaching."[22]

The mid-summer meetings brought out crowds of people and it was reported that the cottages on the grounds had to be opened earlier than usual. "When the Assembly began it was with a settled community. The work of July had filled the atmosphere with high thoughts and enthusiasm. The Assembly found an established esprit de corps."[23] The August lectures were particularly exciting for the Chautauqua faithful. "The broadest freedom was given on these occasions to the speakers. 'I never padlock any lips on this platform' was the motto which the presiding genius announced to his audience."[24]

In addition to the popular lectures, dozens of classes were conducted in such subjects as elocution, penmanship, typewriting, geology, and forestry. The summer assembly at Chautauqua was a remarkable amalgamation of secular education and religious enthusiasm. Year after year the mother assembly attracted thousands of teachers, ministers, politicians, and vacationers to the shores of Chautauqua Lake for "concerts, entertainments . . . and philosophical, scientific, and literary lectures in progressive courses. . . ."[25]

During the 1880s and 1890s there developed hundreds of federated regional Chautauqua assemblies which constituted the third major element of the popular Chautauqua. Vincent, with seemingly undying energy, every summer traveled around the country visiting the loosely associated but loyal gatherings. The regional assemblies greatly resembled those of the "Mother Chautauqua," and in 1885 the *Chautauquan* gave the following report from the West:

The Nebraska Sunday-School Assembly Grounds consist of one hundred and nine acres on the banks of the Blue River, at Crete, Nebraska. Its first session was held in that town in July, 1882, under the direction of Rev. J. D. Steward. Last year a splendid tract of land was donated to the assembly. It extends along the river bank with admirable opportunities for boating, and contains a beautiful grove and ample grounds for buildings, walks, drives, and other purposes. Two lecture halls and a dining hall have already been erected, and some hundreds of tents provided; while a Normal Hall, several cottages and other buildings are proposed. Dr. John H. Vincent . . . will be present and give lectures. Others who have had wide experience in literary pursuits will give their counsels on the ways of spending time most profitably in reading and study for the people. A course of musical instruction will be given by Prof. J. E.

Platt. Prof. W. F. Sherwin will give a lecture and conduct concerts.[26]

The educational system which came to be known as Chautauqua was not without its critics. The most frequently heard criticism was the charge of superficiality. A reader of the *Nation* called false the institution's aim

> of surveying intelligently the ground traversed in the average four years' college curriculum of study. This is expected of people of relatively mature minds, engaged in the active business of life, to spend their time upon the general *disciplinary* course which we think suited to boys of sixteen to twenty, who devote their whole time to study. What can be the result of a year spent upon this set of books but an intensification of the American fault of pretentious superficiality.[27]

Vincent in *The Chautauqua Movement* (1886) acknowledged the charge and responded with vigor:

> Superficial it is, and so is any college course of study. The boy who stands at the close of his senior year, on Commencement Day, to receive his parchment and whatever honors belong to him, who does not feel that his whole course has been superficial, will not be likely to succeed in the after-struggle of life. But superficiality is better than absolute ignorance. It is better for a man to take a general survey, to catch somewhere a point that assists him; for the man who never takes a survey never catches the point in which dwell the possibilities of power for him. By this superficial view he develops taste and power. When you sow seed, it is not the weight of the seed put into the soil that tells, but it is the weight of the harvest that comes after.[28]

Chautauqua was also criticized for publishing and promoting its own books. The editor of the *Nation* led the attack:

A weak side of this interesting system is its manufacture
of special text-books which are subject to the limitations of
production to order as opposed to spontaneous and com-
petitive production. . . . As we have pointed out in these col-
umns, a Chautauqua text-book in United States history ends
deliberately with the war of 1812! The sort of book-reader
this preparation should evolve is one we have heard tell of
who never read a book less than 2,000 years old, and had
not got down to Paul and Silas yet.[29]

Replying to the *Nation*'s editor, a Chautauqua student
of economics cited Professor Richard Ely's text, *An Introduction to Political Economy,* and stated that Ely in his
preface suggested the book would "excite the readers' curi-
osity, and lead them to continue their economic studies."
The impression Ely left according to the student was: "I
do not so much feel that I really know a great deal about
political economy as that I am in a position to learn something."[30]

Critics notwithstanding, Chautauqua thrived for many
years until the automobile, movies, radio, and formal educational institutions distracted its isolated students. Perhaps
no other phenomenon in American life generated the enthusiasm and the active participation of the public to the
degree John Vincent's Chautauqua did. The missionary
spirit which permeated the early decades of the Chautauqua movement was not a product of narrowly defined doc-
trine. The movement embraced a wide range of religious
groups, including Catholic and Jewish Chautauqua organizations. The curriculum of Chautauqua was liberal and the
subject of religion was treated in historical context much
as the universities do today. Self-improvement through enlightenment was the institution's underlying theme.

Some of this enthusiasm infiltrated the early days of extension as we shall shortly see, but the intensity enjoyed by

Chautauqua could not be sustained indefinitely and by the first decade of the twentieth century the momentum of higher adult education had shifted from spontaneous, informal organization to formalized institutions of higher learning.

University Extension in England

While Chautauqua was stimulating thousands of adults with its educational activity in America, the universities in England were developing off-campus programs aimed at the working adult population. This English development was formally termed university extension. Modern literature in adult education generally identifies the period from 1873 to 1890 as the formative era in English university extension, and in fact, great development did take place at this time.

The growth of extension during those years, however, was not without precedent. An earlier movement which occurred in the 1840s and 1850s related to proposals calling for major reform of the two great universities, Oxford and Cambridge.

This earlier conception of University Extension was much broader in its scope than the later one. It was not principally -.. concerned with the extension of university teaching to part-time students, whether living in or outside the university centre itself, but rather with enabling categories of students hitherto excluded from the universities to be admitted to them. In particular it aimed at the abolition of denominational tests for university education and the admission of women to Oxford and Cambridge. More generally, it recognized the need for the development of higher education to meet the social and industrial situation created by the Industrial Revolution—a recognition which had already, before the middle of the century, helped towards the establishment of London University and Owens College, Manchester. . . .[31]

The pressure for university reform over the years resulted in modification of the great English universities. The religious tests were altered in 1854 and finally abolished in 1871, the Oxford and Cambridge local examinations were introduced in 1857, and during this period colleges were founded for women and facilities were provided for other traditionally noncollegiate students.[32] At the same time a number of newer colleges were established in growing metropolitan areas which made provision for adults, chiefly through evening classes and lectures.

What has been described as modern university extension in England began, however, at the University of Cambridge in the year 1873. Extension arose, according to Thomas Kelly in his *A History of Adult Education in Great Britain*, from two specific demands: "One, to which the large audiences at lectures of the type given by Ruscoe and Hurley bore witness, was for university education for working men. The other was for university help in the higher education of women. This latter was in itself part of a much wider demand for a thorough-going reform of English secondary education. . . ."[33]

The pioneering work in university extension in England was done by James Stuart, a fellow of Trinity College, Cambridge, and later professor of mechanics and occasional member of Parliament. In 1867 Stuart gave four lecture courses in Leeds, Liverpool, Sheffield, and Manchester to audiences comprised chiefly of women and teachers. For each case, these courses consisted of eight lectures. Within the following five years, comparable courses were being offered in other parts of the British Isles. In response to the demands of workingmen, Stuart was also lecturing to railway workers under the auspices of the mechanics' institute.[34]

During this experimental period between 1867 and 1872, Stuart developed three features which came to be associated with university extension: the printed syllabus, the written work, and the class discussion. The origin of the written work in connection with lectures occurred almost by accident. When Stuart started his courses it was considered improper for a young male teacher to directly exchange oral questions and answers with young ladies in the audience. As a result, written questions were distributed in advance which required written answers.[35]

While Stuart had expressed his ideas as early as 1866 on circuit-riding professors, in 1871 he appealed to the University of Cambridge to formally initiate such an effort. Education was demanded by the people, he contended: "I believe it is incumbent on us to supply it, . . . and I believe that some such system which will carry the benefits of the University . . . with respect to the education of the country that it has hitherto held, and to continue in its hands that permeating influence which it is desirable that it should possess."[36]

In response to the appeal made by Stuart and his supporters, the university organized a series of local lectures which began in the autumn in Nottingham, Leicester, and Derby, three courses being offered in each location. Receiving favorable response, additional lectures were offered in the spring of 1874 with attendance averaging in excess of one hundred persons a lecture. University extension at that point became a permanent fixture at Cambridge and Stuart was appointed the directing secretary of the program.[37]

At the University of Cambridge the following formal procedures, based on Stuart's early work, were first published in 1873:

(1) Each course consisting of weekly lectures accom-

panied by weekly classes extending over a period of twelve weeks, conducted according to the following regulations: The teacher to remain in the lecture room for some time after the conclusion of each lecture and class in order to answer questions or solve pupil difficulties and to give advice as to the reading of textbooks and other means of efficiently studying the subject.

(2) Each lecture to be accompanied by a syllabus distributed to the pupils and by questions. Those who desire to answer these questions to do so in writing at home, and to be at liberty to submit their answers to the teacher for correction and comment.

(3) The class in each subject to be formed only from among those who attend the lectures in that subject, and to consist of those who are desirous of studying it more fully. The class, at the discretion of the teacher, either to take up the subject of the lectures or cognate subjects bearing directly thereon and necessary for the better elucidation of the subject of the lectures. The teaching in the class to be more conversational than that in the lecture.

(4) Written examinations to be held at the conclusion of each course by examiners appointed by the syndicate, open to any pupil who has attended the course; and certificates to be granted to the candidates demonstrating sufficient merit in these examinations.[38]

The cost of the extension service, as defined at Cambridge, was to be charged to the local community, and this expense was generally passed on to the participating student. A Cambridge circular outlined the expenses which might be expected by any one community for a single course (which included one lecture and one class a week) for a term of from ten to twelve weeks:

(1) A sum of forty-five pounds payable to the university for teaching.

(2) A fee of two pounds for the examination at the end of the course. This fee to be divided equally among the towns which have a course in common.

(3) The share of traveling expenses of the lecturer to be divided among the towns associated in securing his services.

(4) The expense of printing the lecturer's syllabi.

(5) A small fee for the use of slides when the course is illustrated with the lantern, or to meet the cost of experiments and hire of apparatus in the case of such subjects as chemistry and experimental physics.

(6) If the same course is given afternoon and evening of the same day, a fee and a half, sixty-seven pounds, ten shillings, is to be charged.[39]

In practice the cost of the regular university extension course varied considerably depending on the traveling expenses of the lecturer and the amount spent for advertising and the hiring of a hall. Frequently lecture and class space was provided by a local educational establishment for no fee at all. Typically during those early years the total cost of a twelve-week course or unit ran about $325. Of this sum, $225 went to the university and about $100 was allotted to advertising and other local expenses.[40]

Once university extension had gained a strong footing in England, Cambridge lecturers were reluctant to give further single lectures, insisting on a course of twelve continuous lectures in one broad subject area. Lyceum lectures were no longer professionally or economically attractive. However, because some communities were unable to sustain a full twelve lecture course, in many cases shorter courses were offered. The university season fell into two terms, each lasting three months, the first running from October to Christmas, and the second from mid-January to Easter. Efforts were made "to arrange for lectures in circuits of towns or districts, so that the lecturer might occupy his time to good advantage, without traveling over wide areas and wasting his time."[41]

Courses were grouped into three general subject areas: (1) literature and history, (2) science, and (3) art appreciation. From enrollment figures literature and history were apparently the most popular of the areas with science being in strongest demand in the industrial and mining communities. The extension lectures were accompanied by a printed syllabus which aided the student in taking notes and reviewing the week's lecture. Over the years, the syllabus grew from a rather simple outline of lecture topics to a document of considerable length.

Herbert Baxter Adams, a noted Johns Hopkins professor who visited England during this period and promoted the cause of university extension in America, commented on the relationship between the University of Cambridge and towns it reached through extension:

> Many towns in England have carried University Extension so far that they now support several courses in a year and thus maintain a kind of local college or university of their own, with an inviting curriculum of study. Such towns or centers of University Extension are in many cases affiliated to the university, and thus become, as it were, local branches of Cambridge. This institution has gone so far in the direction of recognizing good local work that a student living at a distance from Cambridge may now become recognized as a "student affiliated to the university." Indeed, an extension student may now be admitted to one year's advanced standing at Cambridge, provided he . . . passes a satisfactory examination in six consecutive unit courses . . . thus embracing a three years' course, and provided also that he pass in two other unit courses, and also in Latin, and one other foreign language, and in the elements of higher mathematics. . . .[42]

Oxford formally started its extension activity a few years

after the pioneering work of Cambridge. Following some experimentation, a fresh start was made by Oxford in 1885 when it made a commitment to the shorter course. Recognizing the problems inherent in the full twelve-week term, Oxford concluded that half a loaf was better than no loaf and embarked upon an extension term of six weeks of lectures and classes. Adams commented at the time: "It [the six-week course] has practically brought University Extension within the reach of every town in England."[43]

The example of Cambridge also prompted university men in London to organize a society for the promotion of extension. The London Society for the Extension of University Teaching, as it called itself, came on the scene in 1875 and represented the cooperative resources of many London colleges and institutes, and was advised by experienced lecturers and administrators from both Cambridge and Oxford. The London society was a coordinating agency which for many years aided the smaller institutions in London in their efforts to serve a diverse audience.[44]

In 1885 Adams predicted continued success for university extension in England for three reasons:

> First, it is revolutionizing popular lectures. Instead of the old system of Lyceum course, which was nothing but a cheap variety-show for an evening's entertainment, there is now continuity of interest and specialization upon a particular subject until the audience really knows something about it. Second, university extension brings the higher education into provincial towns without the necessity of endowing colleges or multiplying universities. For a few hundred dollars each year every town and district union in England can have the university system at its very doors. Third, this system strengthens all local appliances for education, whether schools, colleges, institutes, libraries, museums, art galleries, or literary societies. It combines with everything and interferes with nothing.[45]

The development of university extension in England, in

Adams' view, was essentially an economic matter. More than simply a missionary or educational crusade, it was a case of supply and demand: "Representatives of labor and capital in England have awakened to the fact that universities are in the possession of a useful commodity called higher education. Men begin to realize that a good knowledge of English history, political economy, social science, literature, and the arts makes for the general improvement of society and the development of a better state of feeling among its members."[46]

Despite the enthusiasm generated during the early years, English extension was not without its problems. Thomas Kelly, in his study of the early period, cites three difficulties:

(1) It suffered from ambivalence of purpose. While pursuing the older ideal of providing university teaching for people unable to attend the university, at the same time it tried to provide general cultural courses which would impart the knowledge and values (as well as influence) of the university throughout the community.

(2) Extension further operated without the support of a clear social dynamic. Whereas during the earliest days, the movement for higher education for women provided such a dynamic, in time this dynamic weakened. With no apparent underlying force to replace the women's movement, a stable local organization became more difficult to achieve.

(3) The principal weakness of extension, however, was lack of money. Except in the case of technical courses which were supported by local authority, the entire cost of the course was shouldered by the local center. This meant that to pay its way the extension lecture had to sell over one hundred tickets. As a result, low-income working class students were discouraged from attending; subjects were often chosen on the basis of their popularity rather than educational value; and the risk of financial loss was so great

it became difficult to organize a local committee of people willing to accept responsibility for the program.[47]

What can be said of the first fifteen years of university extension in England? Several key characteristics emerge that can be identified:

(1) Extension work at Cambridge and Oxford was an institutional effort with supporting administrative structure. In the metropolitan London area, extension work from an administrative viewpoint was a cooperative effort and promoted chiefly by a single coordinating agency.

(2) The curriculum of extension included both the cultural and practical arts, with the emphasis on the cultural.

(3) The student body reflected a broad cross section of the English population with the financial arrangement favoring the middle class in general.

(4) Geographically, extension reached most of the small and medium-sized communities in England.

(5) The expense of extension fell upon the community and was typically passed on to participating students.

(6) Extension work was an attempt to make adult learning more systematic and continuous.

(7) As methods of instruction, the lecture, class discussion, examination, papers, syllabus, and certificate were widely used.

Early Extension Activity in America

As university extension gained a footing in England during the 1870s and 1880s, it attracted the attention of American educational leaders and the popular press as well. John Vincent of the Chautauqua Institution visited England in 1880 and again in 1886 to observe the movement. In 1885 Herbert Baxter Adams came back to America from England and reported: "There is a remarkable movement in

England towards the higher education of the people. . . .
Sooner or later we shall see the movement sweeping
America."[48]

The movement, in fact, did sweep America, and it did
so in a remarkably short period of time. Impressed, as he
was, with the apparent effectiveness of university extension
in England, Adams became a leading promoter (as well as
reporter) of extension activity in America.

Unlike Vincent, Adams had enjoyed formal schooling
in both America and Europe. An offspring of the colonial
Adams family, he attended Exeter and in 1872 graduated
at the head of his class from Amherst College. After teaching in a private seminary for one year, he went abroad and
studied history, political science, and economics, receiving
his Ph.D., *summa cum laude,* from the University of Heidelberg in 1876. He returned to America and began a life-
long teaching appointment at the newly organized Johns
Hopkins University. While his importance to the extension
movement will become apparent in the following pages, he
is perhaps best remembered for the introduction of the
seminar method in the instruction of history, for his training of such scholars as Frederick Jackson Turner and
Richard T. Ely, and for his editorship of the *Johns Hopkins
Studies in Historical and Political Science.*[49]

Aside from the Chautauqua effort, university professors
had been sporadically involved with extensionlike activities.
As previously pointed out Benjamin Silliman's science lectures earlier in the century had been very popular in New
England. In addition both the teachers' institutes and farmers' institutes called upon members of college and university faculties for lectures on subjects of special interest to
those groups. In 1873 Louis Agassiz conducted a summer
school of zoology at the Penikese Island for the "practical
training of young naturalists." During its two years of oper-

ation some of the better-known American professors of natural science were trained at Penikese.[50]

From its first year, 1876, Johns Hopkins University offered public lectures in the Baltimore area. While this offering was not called university extension, Hopkins invited professors from other colleges to give courses of lectures to which the public was admitted. Adams reported that courses were offered by the university for the benefit of art students, school teachers, lawyers, physicians, clergymen, bankers, and businessmen. A course might have consisted of as many as twenty lectures with a printed syllabus. Audiences ranged from one hundred to seven hundred persons and frequently courses were given in the lecture rooms of the Peabody Institute. In 1879 Hopkins attempted to attract the working people of Baltimore to popular lectures by presenting a course of twelve "lectures for the people" in one of the industrial neighborhoods. The lectures were given by Daniel C. Gilman, president of Johns Hopkins.[51]

The first attempt to consciously introduce lecture courses along the lines of English university extension occurred in 1887 at Hopkins.

> In the winter of that year there began in individual ways the development of two kinds of extension work: (1) local and (2) itinerant. The local work was done in connection with church societies, educational institutions and industrial neighborhoods, workingmen's guilds, and labor unions. A cooperative course of 12 "lectures on the progress of Labor" was given by twelve Hopkins graduates under the leadership of a university instructor. The entire band of lecturers traveled around the Baltimore circuit, each man repeating his one lecture in several different localities. . . . One of the most interesting results of this local work in Baltimore has been the institution of what might be called missionary courses. Many young clergymen and associate pastors have taken courses of graduate instruction at Johns Hopkins, and

some have organized lecture courses in connection with church missions, young men's guilds, Epworth Leagues, etc.[52]

In the West higher education had reached the people at the University of California where professors were expected to give community lectures in the San Francisco area. It was the policy of the state university in Indiana to provide the local lyceums with lecturers.[53] These and other efforts at the time were essentially fragmentary and did not reflect the influence of English extension.

During the year 1887, at the same time he was promoting extension lectures at Johns Hopkins, Adams attended the national conference of the American Library Association which was held in the Thousand Islands' of New York State. At that meeting he described the extension movement in England and exhorted libraries in the United States to open their facilities to the itinerant university lecturer. In a letter to the *Springfield Republican*, Adams summarized his Thousand Islands' address and stated: "Every great public library should become, in its own field, a people's university, the highest of the high school in the community. It should be the roof and crown of organized public instruction not only for existing schools, but also for the graduates of schools, for studious persons already past the school age, whether in the higher or lower walks of life."[54]

Stimulated by Adams' address at the conference, J. N. Larned, the head librarian of the new Buffalo Library, took up the cause. Corresponding with Adams on the mechanics of instituting a lecture program at the library, Larned then floated a trial balloon in a letter to the *Buffalo Courier* in the fall of 1887. After describing his discussion with the Johns Hopkins professor, Larned asked:

The question now is: are there forty or fifty people in

Buffalo, both sexes, young and old, capitalists and workmen together who care to pursue systematic courses of reading, study, question-asking, question-answering, and discussion on this subject, under competent guidance, for a few weeks during the coming winter, and pay, say $4 or $5 for the whole of it? Next: are there 150 people more who will attend the course of twelve lectures, simply, and pay ten cents for each lecture? Finally, inasmuch as it is necessary to be sure of meeting expenses if the course is undertaken, can we get a guarantee fund of about $200 subscribed, to be drawn upon if the course fails to be self-sustaining? I would like to hear from those who feel an interest in Professor Adams' proposal and who can reply in part to either one of the three questions above.[55]

The response to his query apparently proved encouraging, for Larned went ahead with his plan. As economics, and "the labor question" in particular, was a popular issue of the day (the period saw the rise of organized labor, strikes, and in the minds of some, anarchy), it was decided to invite Dr. Edward W. Bemis of Springfield, Massachusetts, to give the course. There was no distinction between the lecture course and the class course; they were offered as one with season tickets priced at two dollars and single admission, twenty cents. In order to attract the working classes, season tickets were offered in the trade unions for half-price.[56] The library in Buffalo was of then-modern design and had a lecture hall large enough to accommodate several hundred people.

A few months after the lecture course concluded, Larned described the experiment:

> The hour from eight o'clock until nine was occupied by the lecturer. Questioning and discussion then followed for another hour. . . . These discussions were partly controversial between different speakers—each being allowed five minutes—but consisted in the main of questions asked and answered, objections urged, illustrative facts cited, and a

general turning inside out of the topic under consideration. They were almost always animated, intelligent, interesting, and instructive. Every shade of opinion was represented in them; for it was a peculiarity of the course that it brought together the most remarkable mixed company of people that we ever saw assembled in our city. The workingmen were fairly well represented, by the leaders of their organizations more particularly; prominent business men and capitalists were usually present; professional men came in numbers; ladies were fully half the audience, and even ladies of fashion found the matter interesting to them; followers of Henry George, disciples of Marx, and other socialistic sectarians were always in attendance, ready to defend their doctrines. Our lecture-room, which seats about 250 people was generally filled, or nearly so.[57]

The following year the Buffalo library sponsored a second course of twelve lectures in American history. Bemis also offered his course in 1888 before an audience of workingmen in Canton, Ohio, and afterward repeated it in St. Louis in that city's public library.[58] Although the subject of university extension was again brought to the attention of American librarians by Melvil Dewey, president of the American Library Association, in 1890 at their conference in the White Mountains, libraries never became firmly established centers for university extension.

Within this climate of growing interest in university-community relations, the most significant developments during the experimental period of university extension in America took place between 1890 and 1892. During this period what had hitherto been chiefly rhetoric was translated into action. The three events which occurred almost simultaneously and attracted the most attention during the period were (1) New York State legislative support of extension, (2) the activity in the Philadelphia area culminating in the formation of the American Society for the Extension of University Teaching, and (3) the placing of the extension division on equal footing with other units at the new University of Chicago.

The State University of New York (an administrative structure which oversaw public higher education in the state) expressed an interest in extension as early as 1888. In January of that year Dewey, the newly elected secretary of State University, presented the subject in conjunction with the pending reorganization of the state library. In July of the same year he again raised the subject at the University Convocation, emphasizing the relationship between libraries and extension. In January 1889, Dewey brought the subject to the attention of the New York State Senate in one of that body's public sessions. The following summer, he again addressed the university convocation pressing the same subject.[59]

The lobbying effort by Dewey on behalf of extension brought results. In July of 1889 the regents of the University of the State of New York prepared the way for state-wide university extension by adopting the following resolutions:

> Resolved, that the Regents recognize as an important feature of the work the extension of university learning and culture to those who are unable to take the regular course in a college or university.
>
> Resolved, that a committee of three on University Extension be appointed with instructions to report to the annual meeting such plans as they may deem practicable and expedient for carrying forward this work, including a plan for lending to communities, for use during University Extension courses, suitable libraries, collections, apparatus and illustrations.[60]

The University Convocation of July 1890 discussed the question of university extension and appointed a committee of university presidents to deliberate and make recommendations to the regents. In a letter of 9 February 1891 the

committee reported its recommendations in four resolutions which are abstracted as follows: (1) while residential
work was preferred, extension of the advantages of the
university to the people was, nevertheless, desirable; (2)
the regents should establish and supervise a state system of
university extension, including not only lectures, but conferences, examinations, and certificates; (3) a central concern of regents should be the maintenance of high university standards in relation to extension; and (4) in order to
maintain high standards, the regents should work through
a committee of state college and university representatives
in working out the details of instruction and examination.[61]

With the recommendations of this prestigious committee
in hand, the regents formally adopted five resolutions, in-
corporating proposals of the extension committee and calling upon the state legislature to make annual appropriations in support of the plan. The culmination of events
came when, after prolonged deliberation, the state legislature passed, by a unanimous vote, the law which committed
New York State to support the regents' proposal:

> 1. To provide for, promote, more widely extend to, and
> bring within the reach of the people at large, adults as well
> as youth, opportunities and facilities for education, the Re-
> gents of the University of the State of New York are hereby
> authorized to cooperate with localities, organizations and as-
> sociations in this state, where such education shall be de-
> sired, and to aid therein by recommending methods there-
> for, designating suitable persons as instructors, conducting
> examinations, granting certificates thereupon, and other-
> wise rendering assistance in such educational work.
> 2. The sum of $10,000, or so much thereof as may be
> necessary, is hereby appropriated from any money in the
> treasury not otherwise appropriated, for the necessary ex-
> penses of carrying into effect the provisions of this act . . .
> but no part of the sum herein appropriated shall be ex-
> tended in paying for the services or expenses of persons

designated or appointed as lecturers or instruments to carry out the provisions of this act. It is being the intent of this act that such expenses shall be borne by the localities benefited.

    3. This Act shall take effect immediately.[62]

While other early educational legislation did not attract the attention of the press at the time, the Morrill Land-Grant Act of 1862 being a notable example, the University Extension Act of 1891 was acclaimed by editors from Buffalo to New York City. Moreover, the press had reported widely on senate and assembly debate during the months prior to passage of the bill.

Passage of the extension act was significant for three reasons. First, it was the first clear commitment formally made by a state to the extension of higher educational resources to the people. Second, beyond enabling a statewide system of extension, it appropriated funds to support the effort. Third, the appropriated funds were to be used in promotion of extension, but were expressly prohibited from being used as direct payment to lecturers. Like the English system from which it was borrowed, the cost of higher adult education in New York State was defined as a community responsibility with the final burden likely to be carried by the student.

The state university immediately put the program in motion and the university extension department in Albany assumed administrative responsibility for promoting and coordinating extension work in the state. The department listed fourteen ways in which it would provide service to those communities and institutions interested in extension.

    (1) *The Information Bureau.* This unit would answer, personally or by mail, questions on all phases of extension work.

    (2) *The Extension Library.* Extension literature of all

kinds was made available to promoters and managers of the movement.

(3) *Publications.* Explanatory and descriptive literature was provided free or at modest cost.

(4) *Organizing.* Expert assistance would be given in selecting subjects, teachers, dates, etc. When desired an organizer could be sent without charge except for travel expenses.

(5) *Supervising.* On request an expert would inspect the local centers and give practical suggestions for a more effective and efficient program.

(6) *Supplies.* Books and forms needed to keep records would be furnished free, syllabi at cost.

(7) *Extension Teachers.* Lists of teachers would be printed and made available to local centers.

(8) *Examinations.* Those who did the required work for the course could be examined and successful students received the certificate.

(9) *Loans.* Printed material needed by centers unable to pay would be loaned during the period of the course.

(10) *Traveling libraries* were available to small centers, distant from a public library.

(11) *Circuit Books and Apparatus.* For materials needed by five or more centers a cost-sharing circuit plan was used reducing each center's expenditure.

(12) *Exchanges.* The Extension Department facilitated exchanges of used materials between centers.

(13) *Regents' Centers.* Those centers maintaining a ten weeks' course under an accredited teacher, with satisfactory class and paper work, were designated Regents' Centers.

(14) *Registry.* The Extension Department solicited reports from local centers to be used for their mutual benefit and for the department's internal and external use.[63]

While New York State was creating its extension division in Albany, the American Society for the Extension of University Teaching was emerging in the Philadelphia area. In February of 1890, Dr. William Pepper, provost of the University of Pennsylvania, assembled a group of interested educators in his home to discuss the possibilities of extension. A few months later, with the aid of Herbert Baxter Adams, the preliminary organization was completed with Dr. Pepper being chosen the president of the Philadelphia Society for the Extension of University Teaching. The secretary of the organization, George Henderson, immediately made a trip to England to observe recent developments there.

At a public meeting held in Philadelphia in November 1890, addresses were given by R. G. Moulton, an experienced English extension lecturer, as well as President Patton of Princeton and James MacAlister of the Drexel Institute. The following month, the name of the organization was changed to the American Society for the Extension of University Teaching and an advisory board was established consisting of numerous prominent university presidents including William R. Harper, president-elect of the University of Chicago. The society proposed to direct its attention to the national movement by collecting information of the various experiments in university extension and publishing a journal on the subject. Additionally the society would establish a staff of lecturers to serve in Philadelphia and surrounding areas.[64]

In July 1891, the society began its monthly publication, *University Extension,* a journal which for five years was a chief source of information for those working in the field. During the early 1890s many regional centers of the organization were established to promote extension and place lecturers where they might be needed. The American Society in Philadelphia normally worked through the regional branch but when this proved impracticable it dealt directly with the local center.[65]

The American Society sponsored the first national conference on university extension which was held December 1891 in Philadelphia. The editor of *School and College* commented on the event:

> The first annual conference on University Extension, which was held in Philadelphia on the closing days of the old year, gave abundant evidence that this form of higher education has received a hearty welcome in America. President Pepper could well assert that every portion of our vast country is genuinely interested in University Extension. Moreover, the interest is not confined to the large class of radicals who welcome every educational novelty. The idea has captured conservatives as well. Membership in the Council of the American Society has already been officially accepted by more than one hundred college presidents. The conference itself was at once an occasion of inspiration and a school of methods for the delegates, who represented an area indicated by the mention of Massachusetts, Nebraska, and Louisiana.[66]

While the American Society worked with established institutions in its effort to bring higher education to the people, another movement in the cities attempted to effect social reform in a more direct manner. The Neighborhood Guild, founded in New York in 1887 by Stanton Coit, initiated reform work by organizing clubs and meeting places in the tenement districts. The guild, through its educational and recreational activities, sought not only to improve conditions of tenement life but to politically organize the poor as well. In organizing the New York guild, Coit and four other university graduates, including Morrison I. Swift, took up residence in the tenement district.[67] The guild was designed as a university settlement where concerned young, wealthy, and educated men and women could live, enlighten, and help the slum dwellers organize.

In 1888 a similar guild was established in Philadelphia

by S. Burns Weston and within a short time it envisioned itself as a social university: "A central institution for social life and higher learning is needed by all members of society, of whatever class, who toil for a living—whether with hand or brain."[68] The Philadelphia guild worked with those American Society leaders attempting to introduce English extension to America. The guild organizers, however, were the activists of the social reform movement, and identified the capitalists as responsible for the condition of the slum dwellers. In regard to the "social disease," as it was called, Swift commented: "I find going to the source . . . unpopular with capitalists. They call it impertinence. It is always impertinent to interfere with the strong to protect the weak. . . . I know of no protection of the weak against the strong that is not considered impertinent, except the protection of our infant industries."[69]

These were strong words, almost revolutionary in their time. They were not typically uttered by those in the mainstream of the extension movement. The American Society was most active during its first ten years of operation, or until about 1900. During that period approximately 180,000 individuals participated in extension courses operated under the auspices of the society.[70]

In 1892 the organization identified four objectives for itself:

> First, it has undertaken to create a University Extension literature which shall embody a discussion of the whole subject of higher adult education . . . a literature which shall explain the workings of the system and shall also extend and deepen the interest in the objects and methods of University Extension.
>
> Second, the Society has undertaken to publish an official organ of the movement, as a medium of communication among those who are interested in the subject in the United States, Canada and Great Britain.

Third, it has undertaken to provide a means for technical training of University Extension lecturers and organizers, which shall give its students command over the special methods necessary to the prosecution of this work, as distinguished from college and university classroom teaching on the one hand, and merely popular education instrumentalities on the other.

Fourth, it has undertaken to carry on a concrete experiment in University Extension teaching, in the course of which a systematic effort shall be made to solve the difficult problems arising at every point, and to collect and formulate the results of its experiments for the benefit of those anywhere engaged in the movement.[71]

As New York State was beginning to extend educational resources to its citizens and as the American Society For the Extension of University Teaching was developing in Philadelphia, the third major event of the experimental period occurred which drew national attention. With strong financial support from John D. Rockefeller, the University of Chicago opened its doors in 1892. As first president of Chicago, William Rainey Harper brought to that school many of the ideas and methods he had introduced at Chautauqua. Harper had been a key figure in the development of home study and correspondence work at that institution during the early 1880s.

Chicago, too, was the benefactor of twenty years of extension teaching in England as well as the vigorously prosecuted work done by the American Society. Nathaniel Butler, an associate of Harper at Chicago, reported: "University extension lectures are primarily suited for that large class in every intelligent community who are not seeking university degrees but who gladly welcome instruction and direction in subjects in . . . which they wish to be intelligent."[72] But to Harper it was clear that there were many prospective degree students who could be reached by correspondence and class work as well. As a result the university extension division "was organized as an organic part of the work of the University of Chicago, and this Division was subdivided into the coordinate Departments of Lecture-study, Class-study, and Correspondence-study."[73] The placing of the separate extension unit on an equal basis with all other units at Chicago represented the first such arrangement at any American university.

The class-study work was offered at the university itself for Saturdays and evenings. Classes were scheduled at the request of any ten interested students during the first year. By the second year, classes were organized for as few as four persons and were given at the university, which was at that time at the south end of the city, the Athenaeum in the center, and the Chicago Academy on the west side.

By 1893 classes were being offered in churches, private houses, and in several public school buildings. Public school teachers made up a large constituency of the classes. Seventy-three courses of study were offered by forty-five instructors in a wide range of subjects, and upon passing examinations students were eligible to receive full university credit for the work. One-half of an undergraduate program and one-third of a graduate program could be satisfied in this manner. By 1894, some nine hundred students were receiving instruction in forty-eight classes outside the university proper.[74]

Like the class-study division, correspondence-study was organized to meet the needs of nonresident students who were aiming toward a degree. As with the class-study, a substantial portion of credit earned through correspondence could be applied toward a degree at the University of Chicago.[75]

While class-study and correspondence-study for degree credit was being established, the university also organized the lecture-study division along the more traditional lines of extension as practiced by Oxford and Cambridge in England, and the American Society in the United States. On the opening day of the university, 2 October 1892, R. G. Moulton, an experienced English extension worker who had been brought to Chicago by Harper, initiated the first of many lecture courses sponsored by that institution. Between October and December of that first year "over 15,000 persons attended the lectures not only at centers in Chicago and its suburbs but scattered over the region extending from Detroit to the Mississippi, and from Milwaukee to Quincy."[76] On the faculty were seven lecturers assigned to the university extension division.[77]

Looking back at the first twenty years of the University of Chicago, Goodspeed commented on the development of extension at that institution:

> At the beginning and for a dozen years the emphasis was on the lecture system. But this system proved expensive. The hearers of the lectures did not become students. It became surprisingly difficult to find suitable lecturers, and, whether finally or temporarily, this feature of University Extension gradually disappeared. The class-study feature developed into University College, which continually increased in usefulness. At the outset the correspondence-study feature was not conspicuous. Its work began feebly, but, at first gradually and then rapidly increased in volume and power. Under the management of its head, Secretary Hervey F. Mallory, it prospered exceedingly, until it enrolled annually above three thousand students, at work in more than three hundred and fifty courses, given by more than one hundred and twenty-five instructors. Every year it became increasingly evident that this department of University Extension possessed very great capacities of expansion.[78]

The major events of the early years, which dominated the literature of the time, were: (1) the establishment of extension by the University of the State of New York, (2) the attempt at national coordination by the American Society, and (3) organization of an equal-status extension division at Chicago. Grattan has shown, however, that a number of other universities recognized the desirability of offering higher education to the people,[79] and table 1 indicates the number of institutions which formally initiated university extension during those early years. None of the universities before the turn of the century went into extension work with the elaborate organization demonstrated at the University of Chicago.

Table 1.

Number of Universities entering Extension Field

1890–1894 10
1895–1899 2
1900–1904 1
1905–1909 3
1910–1914 8
1915–1919 8

Summer Sessions

As the nineteenth century came to a close, a second strain of higher adult education was beginning to emerge. The summer session, however, did not enjoy anything like the attention given to university extension.

Though the roots of the summer session have been traced back before the Civil War by some writers, the summer work at Chautauqua is generally pointed to as the first attempt at systematic summer study. The early focus at those Chautauqua meetings was the training of Sunday school teachers. In a short time, however, the operation expanded to a summer teachers' retreat for the benefit of secular teachers as well.

At about the same time a few university professors were experimenting with summer classes especially in the sciences, the work of Agassiz being referred to earlier. The development of the early summer school came not from the impetus of the scientific-laboratory movement, however, but from the need to offer additional schooling for teachers. By the 1870s public primary schools were widespread and the public high school was about to emerge. The situation clearly called for additional teachers with formal professional training. The teachers' institute evolved about 1875 into the normal school and by 1885 the summer normal was well established. By 1890 summer normals were available to teachers in a majority of states.[80]

Following the example of Chautauqua a number of private organizations sponsored summer schools for teachers in the 1880s and 1890s. In 1891, some five hundred teachers from thirty-four states attended the National Summer School held in Glens Falls, New York.[81]

During the same period the colleges and universities began offering limited programs for teachers during the summer months. Harvard in 1874 scheduled courses in botany and chemistry for teachers, and two years later teachers came to Bowdoin College for summer work. The Universities of North Carolina and Wisconsin followed in 1887.[82] Summer work was also offered to students in academic difficulty during this period, but there is little evidence that this was any more extensive than tutorial work. The remedial aspect of the early summer session has not been adequately studied, but evidence presently available indicates teacher training dominated the movement for summer offerings.

One of the University of Chicago innovations in addition to the extension division was the year-round calendar. The use of the four-quarter system at Chicago, though not widely emulated, nevertheless gave a certain respectability to summer study.[83]

By 1897, however, the summer session curriculum was already beginning to expand. Cornell offered a six-week course of three lectures daily to students of law who were preparing for the bar exam. In addition to the liberal arts and teacher education subjects, Ohio State University scheduled a course in librarianship, as did the University of Wisconsin.[84] In 1900 the extension teaching division in its report to the regents of the University of the State of New York declared, "The marked tendency of recent years continues without change. The summer school has won its place as a permanent factor in American education."[85] One hundred eighteen schools were reported that year to be offering study in the summer.

In discussing summer schools toward the end of the century, a report to the regents commented on status and trends:

> While it is possibly true that the total number of summer schools is not increasing, observation shows that opportunities for satisfactory work during the summer are becoming more general, while the accompanying equipment is of distinctly higher quality. There is a growing tendency to establish the summer session of the university, following the liberal example of Chicago University. Even when the university does not continue its regular sessions, instruction is often given by individual members of the faculty. . . . In almost every summer school special provision is made for teachers, and this is to be expected since they, more than any other class, are dependent on the long vacation as their only opportunity. Unfortunately for the teaching profession, many teachers are so exhausted mentally and physically at the end of the year's work, that any exertion during vacation would be too great a tax.[86]

In reviewing development of higher adult education,

then, the twenty-year period beginning with Chautauqua in the mid-1870s and ending with the early activity of the American Society and the University of Chicago were years of great enthusiasm, missionary zeal, and rapid expansion. After 1895 this enthusiasm faded, and with it, expansion subsided. A blight, as Grattan termed it, had worked its way into higher adult education.

The American Society journal, *University Extension,* was replaced by the *Citizen* in 1895. Three years later the society ceased journal publication entirely. Whereas ten universities had formally assumed extension teaching from 1890 to 1894 (see table 1), the ten-year period which followed saw just three more institutions enter the field. Reasons for the decline are not altogether clear. Adams suggested five conditions which adversely affected the movement: (1) the scarcity of lecturers capable of dealing effectively with adults, (2) lack of money, (3) lack of time and energy of university people who placed traditional campus duties before extension, (4) the administrative subordination of extension to campus activities, and (5) the competition of cheaper educational opportunities.[87]

In their review of university extension in America, Woods and Hammarberg were somewhat more critical:

> Perhaps the fundamental reason [for the decline] was that the initial enthusiasm was not accompanied by the thorough planning which experience has proved is necessary to initiate and carry on any Extension programme. There was also probably too much dependence on inspirational lectures . . . [other reasons were] inflexibility of much university organization; unwillingness to adapt university methods to needs and training of adults; insistence that programmes adhere to strict university academic standards; lack of financial support; lack of suitable university faculty members to carry the extra burden of travel and teaching; greater claims of academic service on the campus; and the

development of less expensive forms of popular education.[88]

A third explanation is given by Grattan, however, who contended that America and England were two different countries which suggested that extension, in an unmodified form, could not hope to endure in America:

> The import required acclimatization before it could hope to finally succeed; as with many plants, it almost died before it really took hold. . . . It was not until the latter years of the first decade of the twentieth century that it was at all certain that university extension could be successfully acclimatized in America. When the job really began to move toward completion, it was apparent that what Englishmen and Americans called "university extension" was as different in the two countries as the birds they both call "robin."[89]

To whatever reasons one attributes the decline of university extension in America after 1895, there is no disagreement among students of the subject that it once thrived. Clearly, conditions in the country were changing, though the connection between those changes and the evolution of higher adult education is difficult to define.

The early extension ideal sought to take education to all social strata, and in the cities the working classes were largely of immigrant stock. As the rise of public schools overlapped the extension movement, access to these schools may have temporarily reduced the demands of adults for the university's services. By the 1920s large numbers of urban workers had completed their public school education, creating a demand for the urban evening college.

In the West, the frontier had closed and while the movement of peoples continued, communities stabilized and educational institutions came into existence. Between 1905 and

1910 a reorientation of extension in the West took place which rekindled interest and led to the reforming of higher adult education in this country. The model for modern extension emerged at the University of Wisconsin. The following chapter traces how this model developed.

4

The Wisconsin Idea

The first decade of the twentieth century was an era of reform in many areas of American life. The progressive spirit permeated the philosophy of governmental administration, emphasizing scientific inquiry, pragmatism, and the utilization of trained experts in positions of importance. At the same time, progressives encouraged and elevated the idea of service to the state. In a sense, a kind of secular evangelism, not unlike the missionary spirit of earlier days, characterized the progressive movement.

Reform mayors were elected in several cities in reaction to the corruption of the urban political machines. In two hundred cities and towns the commission plan replaced the mayor-council system by 1912. In statewide politics, progressive governors La Follette of Wisconsin, Cummins of Iowa, Hughes of New York, Johnson of California, Folk of Missouri, Smith of Georgia, and Wilson of New Jersey were elected.[1]

In 1903 the direct primary was initiated in Wisconsin, and by 1915 all states had adopted some form of the direct primary. After 1900 many states changed their constitutions limiting the power of the legislature and increasing executive influence. States created "commissions of nonpartisan experts for regulatory railroads, insurance companies, and utilities."[2] In 1910 the state of Washington, following the example of Wyoming, granted the vote to women.

The decade saw reform carried to the national level as well. Stimulated by increasing agitation in the popular press, trust-busting became a major issue of the period. Significant pieces of legislation were enacted during the Roosevelt era protecting the public against the abuses of the giant corporations.[3]

Within this climate of reform, the state of Wisconsin became "an experiment station in politics, in social and industrial legislation, in the democratization of science and higher education. It [was] a laboratory in which popular government [was] being tested in its reaction on people, on the distribution of wealth, on social well-being."[4]

Wisconsin during those early years of the twentieth century had a highly diverse cultural population. In 1900 the state had approximately two million residents of whom five hundred thousand were foreign-born and another one million had at least one foreign-born parent.[5] One hundred thousand were unable to speak English. The Germans and Scandinavians were the largest of these groups, which along with the resident European stock, composed the predominantly rural Wisconsin population. These groups from Northern Europe brought with them a tradition of support for popular educational institutions, ranging from the German Realschulen and Gymnasia to the Danish folk high schools:

Primarily hard-working and efficient farmers, [these] groups represented a tradition of orderliness, of respect for the expert, and of devotion to progress through orderly procedures. German industrialists and Norwegian political leaders carried these traits into their fields of influence. Various smaller groups also contributed from their European heritage to Wisconsin's cultural growth. . . .[6]

The roots of the university-state relations were formed during the 1880s and 1890s. In addition to the attempt to establish English-style extension about 1885, the University of Wisconsin had been instrumental in the agriculture shift from grain to dairy farming, a transition which proved profitable to the people of the state.[7] The impact of university participation in the affairs of Wisconsin life during this period was modest, however, in view of developments which were to occur during the progressive era.

The formal reorganization of the extension division of the University of Wisconsin began in 1906–1907 and the groundwork for that reorganization was laid during the years Robert M. La Follette was the governor of that state, 1900–1906. The Wisconsin Idea, insofar as higher education was concerned, was of two distinct strains. On one hand, it involved the utilization of faculty by state and municipal governments to make more efficient and generally improve their operations. In addition, it meant the extension of university resources directly to the people distant from Madison. In both cases, whether direct or indirect, the Wisconsin Idea was an effort which was to benefit the citizens of the state.

La Follette was a graduate of the University of Wisconsin and laid the foundation for state utilization of university resources when he frequently called upon the university's professors for advice in developing and implementing his reform program:

While I was governor, I sought the constant advice and
service of the trained men of the institution in meeting the
difficult problems which confronted the state. Many times
when harassed by the conditions which confronted me, I
have called in for conference President Van Hise, Dr. Ely,
Professor Commons, Dr. Reinsch and others.

I made it further policy in order to bring all the reserves
of knowledge and inspiration of the university more fully to
the service of the people, to appoint experts from the university wherever possible upon the important boards of the
state—the civil service commission, the railroad commission
and so on—a relationship the university has always encouraged and by which the state has greatly profited. Many of
the university staff are now in state service, and a bureau of
investigation and research established as a legislative reference library conducted by Charles McCarthy . . . has proved
of the greatest assistance to the legislature in furnishing the
latest and best thought of the advanced students of government. . . .[8]

Though individual faculty efforts were too numerous to
list comprehensively, labor and industrial expert Professor
John R. Commons helped draft the bill which was to create
the Industrial Commission on which he later served. T. S.
Adams assisted in writing the state income tax law and
later served on the tax commission. As one observer commented: "The University of Wisconsin has become a kind
of 'consulting engineer' in the public life of the state."[9] A
university poet, William Ellery Leonard, spoke of the "twin
domes of law and learning" a mile apart in Madison.[10]

Perhaps the most important link between university personnel and the state during the La Follette years was
McCarthy's legislative reference library. Though not a formal agency of the university, the library aided the legislature in making more systematic the drafting of bills. It
collected and indexed all materials, including newspaper
clippings, it could secure on state and national legislation.
In his account of those years, *The Wisconsin Idea,* McCar-

thy commented on the reference library: "It was comparatively easy to get laws and court cases but it was far more difficult to find how these laws were administered, to discover the weaknesses in them and to note as far as possible how they could be adopted to use in this state."[11] The reference service was expanded to include trained research personnel and in 1907 the library began actually drafting bills for the legislature, a feature which led critics to deride the library as a "bill factory."[12]

Before this link between the university and the progressive state administration was forged, in 1902 the university president, Charles Kendall Adams, died. His successor was to have a profound influence on the development of university extension at Wisconsin and state universities throughout the land.

Charles R. Van Hise had been a fellow student of La Follette's, "the outstanding genius of our class of 1879,"[13] remarked the governor's widow many years later. Science and mathematics were his early special interests. Van Hise and La Follette were close friends for many years after their graduation. During the 1890s, while he was professor at Wisconsin, Van Hise was also on the staff of the University of Chicago as an extension lecturer.[14]

Upon President Adams' death, a committee of five members of the board of regents had been appointed to recommend a successor. Two of the five nominating members had been appointed by La Follette. Two names were proposed, Van Hise and Dr. E. A. Birge, the acting president. Van Hise was considered a thinker who was direct in both speech and action. Some of the regents were reluctant to appoint him, however, on the grounds that he lacked "oratorical gifts and urbanity." In the end the regents voted eleven to three for Van Hise, and the state press spoke favorably of the appointment.[15]

The Van Hise philosophy of democratic higher education

was apparent on the eve of extension reorganization at Wisconsin. Addressing the first conference of the National University Extension Association in 1915, Van Hise reflected back to the early days of his administration and the influences which led him to his view of an expanded role of the state university:

> . . . utilizing the opportunity to carry out knowledge to the people will be an advantage rather than a disadvantage to the growth of the university. But this should not be its purpose; the purpose should be simply that of service. This idea was fully clarified in my mind when Ward's Applied Sociology (1906) appeared. Ward there proved that the greatest loss which we as a nation suffer is loss of talent. Talent is not the heritage of the rich, but is equally the heritage of the poor. It should be the aim of University Extension to find the way for the boy and girl of talent, whatever the place of birth, whether to tenement . . . or to mansion . . . , so that the states and the nation may have the advantage of his highest efficiency and at the same time make possible for him the fullest and largest life.[16]

Van Hise then went on to consider the university's obligation to those who were not uniquely talented, the average man:

> It should also be the aim of extension to assist the ordinary individual as well. . . . If society were perfectly organized, each individual would have an opportunity to develop to the fullest degree the endowments given to him by nature whether they be large or small. Doubtless this will never be accomplished fully, but it should be the aim of extension to assist every individual in this direction. This then is the purpose of University Extension,—to carry light and opportunity to every human being in all parts of the nation; this is the only adequate ideal of service for the university.[17]

Leading up to the reorganization of extension, the Uni-

versity of Wisconsin had been for several decades involved
in farmers' institutes, short courses dealing with agricultural
problems, lectures, and a summer school.[18] When Van
Hise addressed a group of fellow university presidents in
1906, he told them that Wisconsin was planning to enlarge
"the scope of regular University extension."[19] His plans
were not yet specific and he spoke only in general terms
about his goals for extension in Wisconsin. Only a few
months earlier, in replying to a question, he had commented, "I have given so little attention to correspondence
work that I am unable to express an opinion upon the point
you raise."[20]

The first formal step in revival of extension occurred
when the regents appropriated $250 and appointed history
instructor Edwin Pahlow to be secretary of the extension
department for the balance of the school year 1905–1906.
In March of 1906 it was announced that extension courses
would again be offered on a wide scale and the regents followed with an appropriation of $2,500 to develop the pro-
gram. Henry Legler succeeded Pahlow as secretary of the
extension department and in July 1906, William H. Lighty
was hired to direct the correspondence department. Lighty
had previously been in St. Louis working in a social settlement house. Frank A. Hutchins, who had been associated
with the Wisconsin Free Library, was appointed field organizer of the correspondence department.[21]

With the encouragement of Legler and Hutchins, in the
summer of 1906, McCarthy of the legislative reference library conducted a study in which he found that 35,000 residents of Wisconsin were paying annually the remarkable sum
of $800,000 for instruction from private correspondence
schools. Encouraged by his findings, McCarthy suggested
to Van Hise that the university had the capacity to do a
better job than the private schools and recommended an
expanded program along those lines.[22] At the same time

McCarthy solicited support for correspondence study from the state's leading citizens and forwarded to Van Hise copies of their letters.

Lighty set about determining faculty thinking on how correspondence work should fit into the academic program and, in early October 1906, a special committee was appointed by Van Hise to consider the role of correspondence work and the number of university credits to be given for it.[23] Two weeks later the special committee reported back to Van Hise strongly supporting correspondence work and proposing that granting credit for academic courses would be beneficial to students even though many of them would not pursue a degree. A student could not earn a degree by correspondence alone and only a limited amount of credit could be transferred to the university.[24]

Shortly thereafter, Van Hise asked for and the regents appropriated $7,500 for the correspondence program the following year. In 1907, after considerable deliberation, the Wisconsin state legislature authorized the regents "to carry on educational extension and correspondence teaching and provided an annual appropriation of $20,000 for support of this work."[25] At the same time state support for farmers' institutes was raised from $12,000 to $20,000.

With strong funding now available, it was the task of Van Hise to select the first director of the extension department. Against the wishes of Legler and McCarthy, Van Hise pressed for a scholar, a man whom the faculty would accept as an equal. In the end, Louis E. Reber, dean of engineering at Pennsylvania State University, was offered and accepted the position. Reber wrote to Van Hise: "the position of Director of Extension at Wisconsin would be developing a new line of education in state universities which I believe in the future is likely to become one of very great importance."[26] Reber had been supervisor of his university's engineering exhibits at the Paris Exposition of

1889, the Columbian Exposition of 1893, and the Louisiana Purchase Exposition of 1903. It was reported that "political developments threatened his position in Pennsylvania and encouraged his acceptance of the president's offer."[27]

With Reber directing the extension division, the correspondence program moved ahead swiftly. The Merchants and Manufacturers' Association of Milwaukee had lobbied the year before in the state capital in favor of extension and initially the university served that organization well:

> Cooperating employers in Milwaukee, Beaver Dam, Wauwatosa, and other cities helped employees pay for extension courses, encouraged continuation of work undertaken, and provided rooms in their plants where students and traveling instructors could meet. The extension courses were basically correspondence work, the lessons being sent to Madison for correction. Circuit-travelling instructors met with the students regularly, however, helping them with problems in elementary shop mathematics, blue-print reading, mechanical drawing and similar subjects. It was this corps of traveling teachers which made the Wisconsin program unique in the correspondence field, and attracted nationwide and even international attention. . . .[28]

While industrial training drew much of the publicity given to the early years of extension under Reber, a broader general extension program, which would ultimately prove more enduring, was being established. Frederick Jackson Turner, a former student of Herbert Baxter Adams at Johns Hopkins and a major figure in American historical scholarship, had been charged with drawing up a plan for the training of teachers, and William Lighty worked on a program "broadly conceived . . . for mass enlightenment and uplift."[29] When general extension correspondence study got underway, the courses were offered for $20 which was payable in installments and covered only instructional costs. Moreover, "Extension efforts made the Division a competitor of the private schools, and even of the state colleges and normals."[30]

The early correspondence study undertaken by Wisconsin students was at an elementary vocational level, in the main. In his address at the first National University Extension Association conference Van Hise conceded this point:

> At Wisconsin the correspondence work differs from that in [the University of] Chicago in that a larger portion of it is vocational. Out of 7,662 students doing correspondence work in 1913–14, 3,481 were carrying vocational courses not of college grade or designed for entrance to college; and 3,296 were doing work of college grade. This vocational work is very largely with apprentices and artisans, who finding their vocational training inadequate (indeed there has been no opportunity to obtain regular vocational training in this country), desire to gain knowledge of the industry in which they are engaged whether it be pattern making, plumbing, machine work, foundry work, etc.[31]

While correspondence study constituted a very substantial part of the new Wisconsin extension program, there were numerous other activities which, in all, made the division unique. The Municipal Reference Bureau was organized in 1909. The bureau operated on the theory "that inefficiency, or even failure in city government is due not so much to corruption . . . as to the fact that honest and capable officials are 'ill-informed,' and do not possess the information and knowledge necessary to the efficient solution of municipal problems."[32] The reference bureau assisted city officials and interested citizens (1) by correspondence, (2) by special reports, (3) by the publication of circulars and bulletins, and (4) by consultation and advice.[33] Much of the bureau's work involved answering questions on city ordinances and legal problems generally. In addition it responded to such problems as water supply, sewage disposal, public utilities, and street paving.[34]

Another type of "general welfare work," as Van Hise termed it, was the organization of the package library service. Since people in the rural areas of Wisconsin did not have ready access to libraries but did, like their metropolitan counterparts, have a keen interest in various social and political questions of the day, the bureau prepared syllabi "which gave in outline the legitimate arguments on both sides of each question, with references."[35] Proud of the bureau's work, Van Hise commented:

> The most burning political questions of the day have been analyzed and sent out to all parts of the state, such as the primary election, the election of senators by popular vote, the commission form of city government, the guarantee of bank deposits, etc.; and yet so fairly have the two sides of each question been represented in the syllabus that there have been no complaints regarding this department.[36]

The package library consisted of from two to 100 articles and was "sent out in response to any request from within the State, whether the petitioner be the school district pupil or the president of the Milwaukee Civic Association."[37] There was no charge for the service and materials could be kept for three weeks. From June 1911 to June 1912, 2,450 library packages were loaned out into 313 communities.[38]

The package library service was just one area within the Department of Debating and Public Discussion. This department, in addition, regularly published such bulletins as *Debating Societies—Organization and Procedure, How to Judge a Debate,* and *Principles of Effective Debating.* From 1913 to 1915 the department distributed over twenty thousand of these bulletins which were sent free of charge to Wisconsin citizens and at modest cost to others in over fifty states and foreign countries.[39] The department also served the people of the state by answering inquiries for informa-

tion by letter: "The task often involve[d] a careful research in the large and excellent libraries in the city, a personal interview with members of the University faculty, of
state departments, or someone else whose advice may have
[been] termed expert."[40]

In order to administer extension service to the people,
the university devised a plan to divide the state into six
regional districts. Each of the district offices was located
in a populous center and had a representative in charge
with a staff of engineering and business instructors as well
as a field organizer. From time to time additional university
personnel were added when special programs so required.
"The Instructors devoted all of their time to teaching in
their respective fields, corrected the written work of their
students, and held conferences with students at the district
office . . . where weekly visits were made."[41]

The field worker was not expected to be passive in his
effort to reach the people of his area. One district representative, Andrew Melville, commented: "At times the district organization must *create a demand* for instruction or
lecture courses or community institutes, when it appears
none exists, and where it is evident there is an urgent need
for such service."[42] Such demand was usually created by
the use of circulars, letters, personal visits, and utilization
of the local newspapers. The ingenuity of one organizer
was reported by Melville:

> Recently one of the men in a district office in a race for
> business with an agent of a commercial lecture bureau, ar-
> ranged by long-distance for two committee meetings in dif-
> ferent cities, some thirty miles apart but having good rail-
> way connections. One committee meeting was for 10:00
> A.M. and the other for 4:00 P.M. of the same day; thus by
> use of the telephone, committees were quickly gotten to-
> gether and two courses sold, aggregating $800.00 the day
> before the competitor of the Extension Division arrived on

the ground. Those of you who have been in the lecture course game, will appreciate the necessity for this kind of prompt action occasionally when in competition with the commercial bureau. . . ."[43]

On the question of fees to be charged to those students utilizing university extension, Dean Reber thought "a boy who has been obliged to leave school to become an earner early in life, even though he may have finished high school, is certainly entitled to continue education at the cost of the State as much as one who attends a state college. . . ."[44] In those communities made up predominantly of individuals with only grade school education and no local access to vocational schools, Reber questioned "whether any fee should be charged them for the Extension training they so much need. . . ."[45] However, for those who took instruction for cultural or vocational reasons, particularly in engineering and medicine, he felt a fee was justified. Reber was grappling with a problem his university could not solve equitably in the moral terms he might have desired. In the end hard economics of self-support forced other considerations to ultimately determine the cost of extension for most institutions.

The variety of activities entered upon by the extension division at Wisconsin were so numerous as to prohibit the full discussion each deserves in the study undertaken here. Perhaps the best summary of the Wisconsin program was given by Dean Reber as he suggested the "legitimate elements" of university extension (in addition to correspondence study). He was actually defining the program he largely helped create:

(1) Debating and public discussion, which includes a package library service maintained as a strictly up-to-date record of the more important local, state, and national issues of the day, and which fosters the formation of clubs

and societies for study and debate on public questions and the spread of public intelligence in matters affecting social and civic progress; (2) a department of instruction by lectures, which secures to the smaller communities of the state advantages similar to those usually available only to the larger cities, primarily educational in aim, but using the lyceum method by which musical and dramatic entertainments of excellent quality are included in its offerings; (3) and a welfare department, comprising many forms of suggestive and constructive helpfulness along the lines of community promotion, such as the community survey and the community institute and exhibits based upon the survey; municipal aid whereby the smaller towns may secure technical instruction and service upon problems of government; social center stimulation; health instruction and campaigns; education and entertainment by means of lantern slides and motion pictures; promotion of interest in community music; and short courses or conferences adapted to the needs of persons engaged in institutional or volunteer philanthropies.[46]

The Wisconsin Idea drew considerable attention throughout the nation. Three important books came out of the period, Howe's *Wisconsin, An Experiment in Democracy,* McCarthy's *The Wisconsin Idea,* and La Follette's *Autobiography,* all of which examined features of the period which made Wisconsin unique. In a magazine of substantial circulation,[47] progressive journalist Lincoln Steffens wrote an article entitled "Sending a State to College" which helped focus the attention of millions of Americans on new developments in Wisconsin.

Growth of Extension Across the Nation

The reorganization of extension at Wisconsin and the publicity which accompanied it were not lost on other colleges and universities, particularly the state universities. "In the years 1910–1919 came the greatest expansion of any decade out of the six of university extension's history."⁴⁸ No fewer than sixteen institutions organized extention work during that period. The degree of support given to higher adult education by the universities during the decade varied tremendously. Table 2 indicates selected institutional appropriations for extension for the year 1913–1914.⁴⁹ The figures do not include fees granted from the services provided.

The appropriations in table 2 did not include monies for agricultural extension, which many colleges and universities had been conducting for several decades to one degree or another. In the year 1914 Congress enacted the Smith-Lever bill which granted to each state $10,000 a

Table 2.

Selected University Extension Appropriations
For the Year 1913–14

University of Arizona	$ 2,200
University of Colorado	3,000
University of California	10,000
Columbia University	104,000
University of Florida	11,500
Indiana University	4,200
State University of Iowa	15,000
University of Kansas	15,000
University of Maine	25,000
Miami University	1,000
University of Michigan	10,000
University of Minnesota	40,000
University of Missouri	25,000
University of Montana	10,000

University of New Mexico	1,000
University of North Carolina	1,500
University of North Dakota	7,705
Ohio University	6,000
University of Oklahoma	7,500
University of Oregon	15,000
University of Texas	39,407
University of Washington	12,500
University of Wisconsin	177,380
University of Wyoming	1,000

year for "instruction and practical demonstration in agriculture and home economics" and the "imparting of information on said subjects through field demonstrations, publications, and otherwise."[50]

Cooperative, or agricultural, extension was a joint effort of the United States Department of Agriculture, the land-grant colleges, and various private farm organizations to solve the problems of rural America. It is not the intent of this study to consider the development of agricultural extension beyond noting that, for many years, service to the farm population was an important feature of many college and university outreach programs. For the most part, the Smith-Lever act freed the university extension movement from this responsibility and allowed what came to be called general extension to develop independently of cooperative extension.

Extension in Minnesota

Following the lead of the University of Wisconsin, her neighbor, the University of Minnesota, also penetrated to the farthest corners of the state through the extension division. Extension centers were established in hundreds of communities. Initially much of the division's effort was directed toward the rural population as might have been expected. Most unique, perhaps, was the development of the University Weeks, an affair which involved the faculty and undergraduates, as well as both university and local agencies.[51] Richard Price, director of Minnesota's extension program, described the university teams that visited twenty-four towns, each giving a six-day program of popular lectures, scientific demonstrations, health talks, concerts, dramatic readings, and plays. The emphasis, he contended, was on educational rather than entertainment features.

> Every afternoon there were two lectures and a short program of music and dramatic readings. The lectures covered a wide range of topics, such as bee culture, legal rights of women in Minnesota, the Panama Canal, pure food and drugs, hog cholera . . . to choose a few at random. There were also demonstrations of children's games, an infant welfare exhibit, and talks on public health. Music of a high order of excellence was interspersed throughout the programs. The evening programs were somewhat more ambitious, consisting of concerts by the University Glee Club and professional companies, a play by the students' dramatic club and illustrated lectures.
>
> Twice during the week, at each town, businessmen at luncheons heard a speaker provided to discuss some subject of interest to commercial clubs or businessmen in general.
>
> Not all the participants were members of the faculty. The resources of the University were used so far as they would go, and then recourse was had to professional readers, musicians, lecturers, and entertainers from the Twin Cities and from outside of Minnesota.
>
> Each town was required to contribute $325 for the week's program, and also to supply the meeting place and to take care of local arrangements. . . . For the $325 the university supplied the attraction and paid their railroad and hotel expenses, furnished the advertising matter in the way

of bills, posters, and banners as well as the tickets, and provided a manager to look after the details and conduct the
program. Of course, it would not be possible to furnish so
much for so little money were it not for the fact that members of the faculty and students donate their services. Even
so the "Weeks" do not pay their own way, but the university is glad to make up the deficit as a contribution to social
welfare and community upbuilding.[52]

Price acknowledged that the University Weeks plan was
"very much like that of a Chautauqua."[53] That such a
program emerged in Minnesota was not altogether surpris-
ing given the fact that George E. Vincent, son of John Heyl
Vincent, founder of the Chautauqua Institution, had been
appointed president of the University of Minnesota in
1910. By that time the serious educational effort which
characterized the original Chautauqua had, in large part,
given way to popular lectures and entertainment, and the
University of Minnesota's new president did not seem in-
clined to reverse the trends.

Who stood to benefit from University Weeks? Price
argued that the university gained a better acquaintance with
the communities it served. It also did "the professor good
to get out of the classroom atmosphere and rub up against
humanity as found in the small town."[54] But most of all,
Price contended, "the community, usually absorbed in
business, experiences a widening of the horizon and learns
to think in terms larger than the local unit and to regard
ideas without sole reference to money values."[55] All this
may well have been true but one suspects there were also
strong public relations motives, as Price himself hinted
when he suggested the University Weeks were a way "in
which the people who support a state university may find
out what it is doing and what they are getting for their
money."[56] Whether the hiring of professional entertainers
and lecturers was in keeping with what we now think of as

the best tradition of American education could be argued at some length.

While the University Weeks was perhaps the most spectacular aspect, extension at Minnesota was developing in other ways as well. Like the University of Wisconsin, the University of Minnesota also conducted a Municipal Reference Bureau,[57] correspondence study,[58] as well as numerous other social welfare programs.

Extension in California

By World War I every state west of the Rocky Mountains had established a state university and all of these state universities had university extension divisions, or departments as they were called in the Universities of Arizona and Utah. In his address on extension activities in the West, Ira Howerth described the program at the University of California as being typical of that region.[59] Acknowledging that the University of California had been primarily training the professional, the scholar, and gentlemen "who did not soil [their] hands with labor,"[60] Howerth went on to say:

> The University Extension idea that we are trying to realize is the manifestation of a much broader movement. We have come to the time when everything must be brought to the test of social utility. The test of a man as well as an institution is the service rendered to society. Through University Extension we are succeeding in counteracting the influence of those who have in the past criticized our State institutions. And we are doing something in the institution itself to develop the social conscience. We sometimes meet the criticism that we are discouraging research; that, with the idea of trying to determine the knowledge that is most worthwhile, there may be less emphasis on research. . . . I simply say with regard to University Extensions in the West that we

are trying to realize the University Extension Idea, the
democratic idea in education, development of a social con-
science, the encouragement of the recognition of the distribution of knowledge as the proper function of a university.[61]

By 1917, however, Howerth found that despite the
growth of extension the university was not without its critics: "There are people in our state who still think the university is . . . an institution established primarily for the
benefit of the rich."[62]

The extension division had been formally organized by
Howerth, its first director, in 1913. Seven bureaus constituted the extension unit: (1) the Bureau of Class Instruction which organized and taught classes outside the
university campus; (2) the Bureau of Correspondence
Instruction which offered courses by mail; (3) the Bureau
of Lectures which provided that service singly or in sequence to communities throughout the state; (4) the Bureau of Public Discussion which gave assistance to groups
organized to discuss general interest problems; (5) the
Municipal Reference Bureau which gave information and
offered assistance in the solution of town and city problems; (6) the General Information Bureau which offered
available information on any general subject; (7) and the
Visual Instruction Bureau which collected and distributed
educational slides, motion pictures, and industrial exhibits.[63]

According to the California extension administrator,
F. F. Nalder, the lack of funds made it necessary to charge
fees for each of the bureau's services. Nevertheless it was
reported that demand was far in excess of the university's
ability to deliver services.[64]

In 1916–1917, in what must have been one of the earliest surveys of such activity, the extension division carefully
analyzed its correspondence program. Of the nearly eight

thousand persons who enrolled, 96 percent were twenty years of age or older, and a majority, 55 percent, were thirty years of age or older. Nalder reported that during one typical month about 25 percent of those who inquired about correspondence specified the desire for help in business, 15 percent wished to advance themselves in technical and scientific work, and 7 percent were teachers interested in improving their professional competency. Other vocational groups, secretaries, lawyers, doctors, and writers, enrolled in lesser numbers. Approximately 60 percent were men. With respect to what may be called cultural studies, women more frequently than men indicated preference in this area, the figures being 60 to 70 percent for women as against 30 to 40 percent for men.[65]

From this Nalder drew four conclusions:

> First, the demand for instruction in industrial and technical subjects dominates. Literary subjects are in a small minority except as regards English. . . .
> Second, there is a wide demand for the presentation of science and technology in simple forms, in terms applicable to industry and understandable by men of little schooling. . . .
> Third, there is a strong demand for instruction in business subjects from workers in business pursuits. . . .
> Fourth, many requests are received for instruction in subjects that are not taught in universities. These subjects have arisen through the development of modern industry and commerce.[66]

The University of California during the early days reduced extension, to a considerable degree, to a commodity it could sell. Cultural subjects had little immediate utility and the university, by its emphasis on client-supported programs, showed little inclination to promote and support nonvocational instruction.

Extension at the University of Michigan

The state university located in Ann Arbor, from the 1850s on, had been known chiefly for its emphasis on scholarly research. It was one of the first institutions in this country to experiment with and eventually incorporate the purpose and method of the German universities during the nineteenth century.[67] In 1911, however, the university entered the extension field. It administered its program through nine bureaus, or subdepartments: (1) the Bureau of General University Education Extension which included extension lectures, extension lectures for special groups, and university extension courses which carried credit; (2) the Library Extension Service; (3) the Department of Public Education Service; (4) the Museum Extension Service; (5) the Municipal Reference Bureau; (6) the Architecture and Civic Improvement Bureau; (7) the Forestry Extension Service; (8) the Engineering Extension Service; and (9) the Public Health Service.[68]

During the early years, over one hundred of the Michigan faculty participated in the lectures given to the general community and special interest groups throughout the state. The university paid the lecturer's fee and furnished advertising materials, while the community was asked to locate a suitable hall and distribute the promotional material. The lecture itself was open to the public at no cost.[69] The aim of the extension program was general rather than professional or vocational education. Though Extension Director William Henderson believed the chief purpose of extension was the welfare of people of the state, he candidly spoke of other considerations:

> Is this desire to render service through university extension unselfish in its motive? I do not hesitate to answer that the desire . . . is a real desire to make the world in which we

live more livable for ourselves and our fellows. I am not blind to the fact, however, that state-supported educational institutions are not unmindful of the fact that, in rendering of public service, they are in the end to be the beneficiaries. The very life and existence of a growing state-supported educational institution depends in no small measure today upon its ability to establish a close and sympathetic relationship with its constituency, that is to say, with the people who not only benefit directly by its work, but who also foot the bills.[70]

Extension at the University of North Carolina

General university extension in the South and Southeast was somewhat less well developed by the First World War than in other sections of the country. In North Carolina a close association with the public schools had represented an earlier type of outreach, the operation of the high schools being regulated through the state university's Department of Education rather than the Department of Public Instruction at the state capital. This same type of close university-school relation existed in Virginia, South Carolina, and in a number of other southern states.[71]

In general, it was reported that extension in the Southeast developed through departments rather than through separate divisions.[72] Extension started at the University of North Carolina through the medium of school literary societies utilizing the package library service of the university. Shortly thereafter Kentucky and Alabama Polytechnic followed along the same lines. A similar development of the lecture system occurred when invitations from rural superintendents requested a speaker or other educational materials. A variety of other programs were organized in the South but were not conducted directly by the university, as they were in other states. A separate library commission

was established in North Carolina in 1909, and similar
agencies emerged in other southern states which offered the
traveling library as a service to the people.[73] In the same
manner, health instruction was offered to the public outside
university channels.

Like extension leaders in other sections of the country,
the director at the University of North Carolina recognized
the dual purpose of his efforts: "I think we have contributed real value to the state and at the same time part of
our work has been purely for publicity effect. We had to
do that to get the institution before the people and show
how it could really serve."[74]

University Extension in the East

The state university in the East, due primarily to the long
tradition of the private college and university, did not domi-
nate higher education as did state universities in the Midwest and Far West. The state university systems and individual universities did, however, conduct extension activities in varying degrees.

The State University of New York during this period was
particularly active in library work distributing over 300,000
slides per year as well as photographic prints, wall pictures,
and books.[75] The same type of activity was undertaken
in Pennsylvania on a somewhat smaller scale. Rhode Island, through its State Department of Education, did considerable work with libraries as well as furnishing "speakers
for various occasions and [promoting] activity through
conferences on sanitation and hygiene."[76]

Like the state departments, individual private and public
colleges and universities were involved in extension work
to one degree or another. In response to a questionnaire
distributed to sixty-five institutions by C. B. Robertson,

director of extension at the University of Pittsburgh, some
thirty-five indicated activity in outreach:

> The most significant thing is the large number of these
> institutions which seem to feel called upon to give outside
> service of some sort or another; in most cases it is limited
> and not well organized, but from some source they have
> been inoculated with the Extension spirit, and have devel-
> oped more or less clearly defined symptoms of service to the
> outside group.[77]

Clark University conducted an annual Children's Institute with a budget of $2,500, a part of which supported a
weekly on-campus lecture series open to the public. Temple
University in Philadelphia offered extension classes chiefly
for teachers, and the University of Pennsylvania offered
work in accounting and finance in four cities. The Carnegie
Institute gave "lectures on request to any organization for
a fee."[78]

Perhaps the strongest extension program of any eastern
university was that of Columbia. An old tradition for extension teaching existed at that school. As early as the
1830s and 1840s it had experimented with courses directed
to "young men employed in mercantile and industrial establishment."[79] During the 1890s lectures were offered to
the public and by the first decade of the twentieth century
courses designed for teachers in the evening, on Saturday
mornings, and during the summer months were a regular
feature of the Columbia curriculum. The development of
extension had a special meaning for James Egbert, the
director of the summer session and evening teaching:

> The experience of the past year has served to indicate . . .
> that Extension Teaching . . . has not only served the com-
> munity well, meeting . . . the educational demands that are
> now most pressing, but has supplied the University itself
> with an agency which has a great value in its own develop-

ment and growth. . . . The aim of Extension Teaching is two-fold. First, to afford extraordinary educational opportunities to an eager community and, second to serve the University by introducing and testing new educational schemes and plans and supplying needed courses without extraordinary demands upon financial resources of the University.[80]

Between 1910 and 1920 the extension curriculum and method of instruction became highly diversified and involved in activity in short-term courses, concerts, cultural subjects, as well as professional training in architecture, dentistry, law, and pharmacy. In 1919 the Columbia Administrative Board approved the inclusion of correspondence study and established for its administration the Department of Home Study.[81]

The specific institutional arrangements discussed in the previous few pages by no means exhausts the list of colleges and universities involved in extension work. They represent an overview of the field as it existed after the statewide scheme for extension was developed at the University of Wisconsin. It becomes somewhat clearer, upon looking at the national field, that by 1915, there was great variety in commitment, institutional arrangement, and type of programming offered.

Wisconsin extension, with strong legislative and dynamic administrative leadership, had reformed its services in spectacular fashion. The influence of the Wisconsin program was felt most strongly by the other state universities, particularly in the Midwest and the Far West. In other sections of the country, most notably the Northeast and Southeast, the influence of the educational reformation at Wisconsin was less strongly felt. The tradition of the strong private colleges and universities of the Northeast and the sparse population of the Southeast worked against adoption of the Wisconsin model in those areas.

While, in a real sense, Wisconsin helped clarify the role of the state university to include service to the public as well as the primary functions of teaching and research, the development of Wisconsin extension by no means unified American higher educational institutions on the question of how much service to the public was sufficient, through what institutional arrangement it should be offered, or what subject matter was appropriate. The chief lasting contribution of Wisconsin, it will be seen, was less as a model or showcase for other institutions to emulate, than as a promoter of institutional re-evaluation. Ultimately the university, more than any other, made service to the public a respectable goal for American higher education.

The strong resurgence of university extension between 1905 and 1915, led by the University of Wisconsin, resulted in the emergence of the National University Extension Association in 1915. For several years prior to that date, Wisconsin's extension division had received letters from "widely separated sources suggesting the possible value of such a conference."[82] As a result of these inquiries a circular was distributed around the country to interested parties "asking for expressions of feelings as to where such a conference should be held and by whom it should be called."[83] The response was overwhelmingly in favor of Wisconsin for both sponsorship and location. Louis Reber was elected president of the association and at the March 1915 conference in Madison, he commented on extension in America:

> That the conference is timely must be generally conceded. The status of University Extension in this country is still more or less indeterminate; its methods, even where most highly developed are to a degree experimental. It is apparent that its scope may be different in every State, yet there are many conditions common to all from which arise problems that are worthy of profound attention, while, as has

been said, the very plasticity that is characteristic of extension in America makes discussion not only desirable but important.[84]

Some twenty-two institutions belonged to the NUEA that first year, all but four of which (University of Chicago, Columbia University, the University of Pittsburgh, and Harvard University) were state colleges or universities. By 1920 membership reached thirty-four institutions and it was reported:

> From fifteen to twenty letters a week have been received by the secretary in regard to Extension and adult education from institutions and individuals not members of the Association. The nature of these inquiries and the character of the institutions concerned indicate that unless this Association opens its membership to a wider circle, new adult education associations will be formed and the leadership of the National University Extension Association seriously threatened.[85]

The warning carried more than an element of truth. In subsequent years a variety of general and special organizations arose which infringed upon the monopoly of leadership NUEA enjoyed during the early years, perhaps the most notable being the Association of University Evening Colleges which emerged in 1939.

The development of numerous professional associations and societies from the 1920s to the 1940s, however, reflected somewhat more than what may have been inferred from the statement of the concerned treasurer of the NUEA in 1920. In fact, the coming period witnessed a significant expansion and change in direction of the higher adult education movement in this country. Chapter 5 will present this development.

5

Years of Growth and Crisis

Having discussed at some length the Wisconsin Idea and its immediate impact on extension in other institutions, I will focus this chapter on the expansion of higher adult education in America from approximately 1920 through the Second World War. While many features of the Wisconsin plan extended into this period, this chapter will be primarily devoted to those aspects which either were nonexistent during the earlier interval or experienced rapid growth between the world wars. In other words, this chapter will concentrate on the details of extension development unique to this period.

Knowles described the era as that of "the greatest expansion and innovation in adult education to date."[1] It was marked by an increasing population which continued its movement from rural to urban areas. The ratio of native-born to foreign-born increased as immigration quotas slowed the rate of incoming peoples. The period was also

marked by crises, recovery from the First World War, the
Great Depression, and the Second World War. In economic
terms, productivity per man increased as the labor force
gradually shifted from the unskilled to the skilled. The
calamity of the depression led to the election of Franklin
D. Roosevelt, and "the traditional laissez-faire policy regarding government's role in economic affairs was reversed."[2]

In the social area, continuing urbanization of American
life was perhaps the most important feature. This progression was accompanied by improvement in transportation
and communications, a higher standard of living, greater
social and geographical mobility, betterment of health conditions, the expansion and coordination of welfare services,
the wider acceptance of recreation as a desirable social
function, and the reduction of racial and religious dis-
crimination.[3]

Within the university structure, according to Grattan,
"by the 1940s university extension had shaken down into
something like a fixed pattern of activities."[4] In a paper
read at the annual meeting of the American Association for
Adult Education in 1940, W. S. Bittner of Indiana University, secretary-treasurer of the National University Extension Association, commented somewhat critically:

> Perhaps I am safe in saying that the thirty or forty years
> of university extension in the United States have completed
> a period in the sense that now there is nothing significantly
> new, no particularly important innovation apparent either
> in the philosophy or the practice of university extension. It
> has a traditional pattern showing little evidence of reshap-
> ing. There are, of course, some changes. One of them . . . is
> presumably a kind of reversion to academic strictness by the
> adoption of such names as University College or Evening
> School in the place of University Extension and the practice
> of designating by fiat certain extension centers as "resi-

dence" centers for degree-credit purposes. Such changes are superficial variations of an old pattern.[5]

In his study, *The Extension of University Teaching,* published on the eve of the Second World War, James Creese contended: "Conventional forms persist. Extension is old enough now to have its own traditions and codes and . . . depart[s] from those only reluctantly."[6] Elaborating on his concern, he wrote: "Those who know the work of university extension best and have the highest hopes of its use in public education are the most conscious of risks of inflexibility and immobility."[7]

Between the two wars, university extension became an accepted, institutionalized form of adult education, comfortable in its ways, and by 1940, it demonstrated little of the enthusiasm for experimentation which had characterized earlier days.

During this period, three developments stand above all others in the evolution of higher adult education: (1) the rapid increase in the number and size of evening colleges, (2) the similar increase in number and size of community colleges which offered services to adults, and (3) the introduction of radio as a tool of extension, used primarily, though by no means exclusively, by the state universities.

The Evening College

As early as the 1920s, various colleges and universities were initiating or expanding their evening offerings. In contrast to the more traditional forms of extension which had already shown signs of stabilizing, the evening college was only beginning to come into its own:

. . . facts seem to justify the conclusion that correspondence

work and extension classes away from the college or university campus were developed prior to, and with greater vigor
than, evening or Saturday morning classes on the campus itself, and that now institutions, especially those located in
centers of population, are realizing that their best opportunities for serving part-time students are right at home in
their own classrooms. Hence, the remarkable increase in
evening and Saturday morning enrollment . . . as compared
to that for other fields of part-time education. Even now,
however, there are state universities and colleges which engage in a considerable program of correspondence study and
extension class work in centers located away from the university campus to the utter neglect of evening school work at
their very doors.[8]

The evening college, to a great degree, resulted from the
rise of the urban college and university. That both private
and state colleges and universities were of urban as well as
rural nineteenth century origin is well known. In addition
to these two types of institutions, however, the municipal
university could also trace its roots into earlier periods of
American higher education.

The first two municipal universities (institutions supported mainly by municipal taxation and maintaining a
four-year bachelor of arts program as well as other departments or schools) were the College of Charleston and the
University of Louisville, both founded in the year 1837.
The municipal university, however, never received benefits
which the state universities enjoyed through the Morrill
Land-Grant Acts. Without strong federal subsidy, growth
of the municipal university was far less spectacular. In
1928, Kolbe identified nine institutions which could prop-
erly be termed municipal universities.[9] A number of other
schools were reported to be receiving partial municipal
support.[10]

Though Kolbe believed the municipal universities were
"in a true sense the product of their environment,"[11] he

nevertheless was not optimistic about their future development:

> In every case, as has been said, the creation of a public university has been due to local conditions, influenced in some cases by the example of other cities. On this basis alone there is no reason to believe that the future growth of this idea in American cities is destined to be anything but sporadic, as has been the case in the past.[12]

In retrospect, Kolbe's assessment was correct. The chief reason for the establishment of the bachelor's degree-granting municipal university, to provide local access to higher education at moderate cost, was precisely the reason for the growth of associate degree-granting public two-year colleges, many of which were to be supported by local funds. With the educational opportunities, particularly those of a vocational nature, being offered by the community college, enthusiasm for the more expensive municipal university facility waned.

While the municipal university experienced no remarkable growth, other urban institutions did. The state and private colleges and universities, particularly the private ones, rapidly expanded in number and in size from the Civil War down to the modern period. Although a variety of factors were responsible for this progress, many private universities were operating with the benefit of substantial endowment, and state supported institutions benefited from the continuing trend toward state responsibility for all levels of education. In the modern era we see this trend extending even to discussion of national responsibility for education.

Like the municipal university, the state and private urban institutions developed evening sessions for the education of part-time students. The private urban institutions, particularly, recognizing the advantages of more thorough utilization of their physical facilities, led the evening college movement. Not only were more evening sessions established in considerable numbers between World War I and World War II (John R. Morton in his study *University Extension* reports fifteen of forty NUEA member institutions alone initiated evening sessions during this period), but the number of students attending those evening sessions greatly increased as well.[13]

Kolbe studied municipal universities in considerable detail and suggested that the University of Akron (Ohio) was typical in its growth. Table 3 depicts the growth of that institution from its inauguration as a public university in 1913. The striking figures in this table are the rapid enrollment increases of evening and extension students, the somewhat slower increase in number of faculty members and day students, and perhaps most importantly, the contrast of faculty growth with nonday student expansion and total enrollment. It should be remembered that the nonday enrollment was not full-time equivalent; that is, many students were taking only one course. Nevertheless, it is apparent that Akron, over a ten-year period, made more efficient use of its faculty either through greater teaching loads or larger classes, or both.

While the total day growth was perhaps atypical due to its transformation from private denominational status to that of a municipal university in 1913 (low or no tuition inevitably brought more students), the wave of evening students was characteristic of many other institutions after World War I and up to the early years of the depression. A second set of figures compiled by Kolbe reveals that cost per student dropped from approximately $264 to $207 between the calendar years 1920 and 1922,[14] precisely during the period of greatest expansion of nonday student enrollment. The Akron example clearly suggested the financial advantage which hundreds of other universities

Table 3.

Growth of the University of Akron*
1913-1925

Academic Year	Day Students	Evening and Extension Students	Summer Students	Total Enrollment	Faculty
1913-14	198			198	23
1914-15	249			249	26
1915-16	283	105		388	27
1916-17	298	447		745	27
1917-18	303	303		606	28
1918-19	454	373		827	31
1919-20	510	509		1019	32
1920-21	555	449		1004	35
1921-22	788	1087	221	2096	45
1922-23	899	1124	332	2355	49
1923-24	1004	1151	359	2514	55
1924-25	1068		325	2389	56

*Adapted from Kolbe, *Urban Influence on Higher Education*, p. 163.

came to enjoy by extending the use of their facilities to evening and summer students.

The National University Extension Association, founded in 1915, was composed primarily of those state institutions which had experimented many years earlier with English extension and then emulated to one degree or another the Wisconsin pattern. About the same time another organization, the Association of Urban Universities, was formed as a result of a conference called by the Commissioner of Education in 1914. The conference was called for "all municipal universities in cities interested in the service of their communities."[15]

According to John Dyer: "By 1915 the problems and programs of the urban universities had become sufficiently differentiated from those of the state university to warrant the establishment of organizations of their own."[16] The association came to be a mix of municipal universities, state universities, and private colleges and universities. Over the years, as Dyer notes, the organization shifted in emphasis:

> Each year at its annual meetings the problems of the urban universities were discussed, and in these discussions adult education came in for its share of time. As a matter of fact, as the years went on the annual meetings might well have been mistaken for meetings of evening college deans, for they were the men who, by and large, were representing their universities instead of the presidents. This was far from what the founders of the Association had in mind. They had envisioned a small, fraternal association of college presidents in which all the problems of the urban university might be discussed, not merely the problems of the evening divisions.[17]

The growth of the urban university was accompanied, then, by a rather distinct separation of day and evening programs. For the most part, the work offered in the evening session tended increasingly to resemble the day curriculum, but from the start, the question of academic credibility was evident:

> Originally much prejudice was manifest in academic circles against any type of evening work. It was felt that such offerings must of necessity be of low grade, since their pursuit was not the main interest of the students engaged. The lax enforcement of entrance requirements in the early years often brought to such courses a hopelessly mixed class of students, of various degrees of preparation, and the resulting mortality was not encouraging to the best effort. Gradually it was seen by the stronger colleges that evening work must be carried on with the same requirements as day work, if success were to be attained. As a result . . . evening

session classes on the campus have been purged of lax methods and procedure, and have gained an academic respectability which is nowadays practically never questioned.[18]

During the 1920s studies relating to the college student and his learning process began to appear with greater frequency. In his observation of the evening college student, Kolbe found they were generally high school graduates who found it impossible to attend college on a full-time basis during the day for financial reasons. Because they frequently worked for a period of time before entering an evening college program they were somewhat older than their day counterparts. The evening students often came from established vocational positions and sought "some special knowledge to aid them in advancement."[19]

The vocational or professional element, particularly industrial, commercial, and teacher education, dominated the evening college curriculum: "This is the distinctive urban side of development, for only in large communities are such students to be found in sufficient numbers to warrant evening session classes of this kind."[20]

Though the vocational courses of the evening session were in great demand and encouraged by employers,[21] liberal arts subjects were not altogether neglected: "Throughout the country, thousands of persons are pursuing evening courses for the arts college degree without any vocational purpose."[22]

As the urban colleges and universities grew in number and in size, the evening session approached or surpassed the day session in total enrollment if not in hours elected. With this development and supported by a growing body of research on learning, attention was given to the special character and motivation of the adult student. An official of the University of Pittsburgh commented in 1928:

The first [of several evening division problems] has to do with obtaining faculty members who are able to relate the subject matter and classroom discussion to the experiences of the adult student. The instructor must talk the language of the students, draw his illustrations from their fields of interest, and in general, relate the subject to their past experiences in such a way that they can see where it fits into their lives.[23]

The evening session faculty was discussed in a paper presented at the Association of Urban Universities Conference of 1928. There Zook reported North Central Association statistics which indicated that 19 percent of evening, extension, and correspondence faculty were "part-time instructors employed for this work,"[24] and that salary compensation for all types of nonday faculty instructors was below that of the regular day instructor.

The evening session by the late 1920s was fairly well established and a rapidly growing segment of American higher education, particularly at the urban universities. Within the field of higher adult education, the evening division was approaching the state extension units in vitality and enrollment. Kolbe reported the thirty-one member institutions of the Association of Urban Universities alone enrolled nearly sixty thousand students in 1927. He further estimated that there were perhaps one hundred thousand evening students in all American colleges and universities, that total being "from 10 percent to 15 percent of the size of the regularly enrolled day student numbers."[25] While the evening sessions growth had been spectacular between 1915 and 1930, there were other developments which were also essentially new and had major implications for higher adult education. In the case of one development, the junior college, impact was felt not only on higher adult education but eventually upon the whole higher educational establishment in America.

The Junior College

The remarkable growth of the junior college since World War II has somewhat obscured the fact that the roots of a separate and independent two-year institution go back well into the nineteenth century. In 1852, in his inaugural address as president of the University of Michigan, Henry Tappan suggested the transfer of some of the lower division work of the university to the high schools. In 1869 W. W. Folwell, president of the University of Minnesota, similarly spoke of the desirability of transferring the "body of work for the first two years in our ordinary American colleges"[26] to the secondary schools. During the 1880s the president of the University of Illinois unsuccessfully tried to interest his trustees in a similar plan.[27]

Apparently the German educational system must have influenced these early efforts. The Gymnasia included general, college-level study (nonspecialized) which characterized much of the American undergraduate curriculum. Tappan, in particular, was an advocate of the German system.

As discussion continued in the educational community for a number of years, the first genuine separation of upper division and lower division work occurred at the then new University of Chicago, a development which has since earned William Rainey Harper the title "father of the junior college." At Chicago the lower division was called originally the Academic College and the upper two years were the University College. Four years later, in 1896, the designations were changed to Junior College and Senior College. This was perhaps the first application of the term "junior college."[28]

Upon successful completion of two years of college work, a student at the University of Chicago, through its Junior College, was granted the degree of Associate in Arts.

In a university report published in 1903, Harper suggested five advantages of such a curricular separation: (1) Many students would find it convenient to give up college work at the end of the sophomore year; (2) many students who would not otherwise do so, would seek at least two years of college work; (3) the professional schools would be able to raise their standards for admission, and in many cases, those who desired a professional education would take the first two years of college work; (4) academies and high schools would be encouraged to develop higher work; (5) and many colleges which did not have the means to do the work of the junior and senior years would be satisfied to operate as lower division colleges.[29]

While the University of Chicago led what for a time appeared to be a trend in the "amputation of the university," pressure was building as well for "many high schools to extend their work upward to include the two years unwelcomed by the Universities."[30] Impetus for the independent junior college may well have come more strongly from the high schools than the universities as President Angell of Yale suggested in 1915.[31] Eells reported that the first such effort by the high schools occurred in Michigan where "the University of Michigan was accepting one year of college work done by the high schools"[32] during the early 1890s.

The first public junior college, Joliet Junior College, was established in 1902, and this event was due essentially to the persuasive powers of Harper. He succeeded in convincing the superintendent of Joliet Schools, his long-time friend J. Stanley Brown, of the merits of two-year college instruction given through the high schools. In 1904, Brown reported that Muskegon and Saginaw, Michigan; Philadelphia; St. Joseph, Missouri; Goshen, Indiana; Joliet, Illinois; and eighteen other institutions across the country were "working out the six-year plan, giving college work in connection with the high school."[33] Thereafter, the two-year college began a rapid rate of growth with both public and private support as seen in Table 4. The expansion of the public junior college was best seen in California. The first

Table 4.

Early Growth of Public and Private Junior Colleges in the United States*

Year	Public	Private	Total	% Public
1915	19	55	74	26
1922	70	137	207	34
1927	136	189	325	42
1931	178	258	426	41
1935	219	302	521	42
1940	258	317	575	45

*Eells, *American Junior Colleges*, p. 18.

public junior college in that state was established in Fresno in 1910. Shortly thereafter others appeared, and when by 1928 California could boast forty-six junior colleges, all but thirteen of them public, the state superintendent of public instruction commented:

> The junior college is with us. In fact, it is so much with us here in California that discussion of its desirability is simply discussion *ex post facto.* . . . It would require a public upheaval to uproot any established junior college in the state. . . . The development since 1921 indicates that the state is now committed to approve the establishment of a junior college in each community that wants the institution, provided the community has students enough to justify it, wealth enough to support it, and a will strong enough to have it.[34]

As early as 1920 it was apparent that the two-year college was on the threshold of national impact on American

education, and Commissioner of Education P. P. Claxton
called a conference of junior college representatives to meet
in St. Louis. Out of that meeting came the American Association of Junior Colleges. The association thereafter met
yearly, at first publishing only *Proceedings.* In 1930, however, the association began publication of the *Junior College Journal,* a monthly which in its early days concentrated
its attention on various college programs around the
country.[35]

The status of community service at the junior college
during the early period is not altogether clear although it
seems safe to say that adult education was considered a responsibility of at least some of the colleges. In a much
quoted doctoral dissertation written at Stanford (1926),
F. W. Thomas defined four basic functions[36] of the two-
year college:

(1)   The popularizing function
(2)   The preparatory function
(3)   The terminal function
(4)   The guidance function

The popularizing function was to give advantage of a
general college education "to high school graduates who
could not otherwise secure it for geographical or economic
reasons; and to give similar benefits to mature residents of
the community."[37] Dean McKenzie of the Detroit Junior
College commented in 1920:

> I think it would be a great mistake to limit the scope of
> the junior college. . . . If democracy is going to be preserved
> by education it will be by bringing education down to the
> masses. There are many intelligent people in large com-
> munities who are capable of profiting by college but who are
> in no way fitted for college according to the typical entrance
> examinations. The junior college ought to offer a large
> number of courses that will appeal to such persons. The
> junior college in large cities is going to appeal to thousands

when it offers courses of this nature and particularly courses
in the evening. This I believe is going to be the saving grace
of democracy.[38]

Such speeches as given by Dean McKenzie had a famil-
iar ring. They could have been and, in fact, were uttered
by university extension leaders for a generation or more before McKenzie made his appeal at the first conference of
the American Association of Junior Colleges.

The Bureau of Education report in 1928 indicated thirteen types of college and university extension activities, all
but one of which, home reading, was undertaken by some
junior colleges:[39]

(1) Correspondence courses
(2) Public information (including package library
    service)
(3) Home reading courses
(4) Publications educational in nature
(5) Class instruction outside of institutions
(6) Public lectures and lyceums
(7) Visual instruction
(8) Institutes, conferences, and short courses
(9) Parent-teacher associations or other club service
(10) Community drama
(11) Community center
(12) Radio
(13) Promotion of debates

The bureau's report did not include formal, on-campus
evening instruction which some junior colleges also offered
to students interested in part-time study.

Adult education in the community college, like that of
the university, was of two general types, vocational and
cultural, although no clear picture emerges as to whether
one strongly dominated the other. Like the four-year colleges and universities, some junior colleges by 1927 had ini-

tiated summer session programs. In 1927 it was reported
that "at least fifty-three junior colleges in eighteen states
had summer schools . . . enrolling almost eight thousand
students."[40]

During the 1930s adult education, however peripheral
in the two-year colleges, became the subject of an occasional article in the *Junior College Journal*. These articles
typically concentrated on specific college programming:[41]
the adult student,[42] or philosophical foundation of junior
college adult education.[43]

Junior college service to the community appears then to
have been realized in various ways and to varying degrees.
For the most part, the public junior colleges resembled the
universities in their adult education activity, particularly
through their evening division work. During the 1920s and
1930s, however, the junior college was still in its early
stages of development. In the years after the Second World
War, the colleges' ardor for community service would become stronger and what had been chiefly peripheral would
emerge as a primary function.

Radio and Higher Adult Education

In addition to the evening college and the junior college,
the period between the two world wars saw another development which seemed destined to play a major role in
higher adult education. For a time, the rapid expansion of
educational radio, especially radio operated by universities,
paralleled that of commercial radio. By 1940, however, the
great promise of extension by radio had not been realized.

In the popular mind, early recollections of radio go back
to 1920 when KDKA in Pittsburgh broadcast the Harding-
Cox presidential election returns. In fact, however, "at least
three state universities (Wisconsin, Minnesota, and North

Dakota) . . . had successfully transmitted both music and voice over the air prior to that date."[44] During the early 1920s radio was considered by extension leaders to be the future tool in the university's link with the public. Between 1920 and 1923 some six hundred radio stations began broadcasting and the American public had purchased two or three million receiving sets.[45]

In 1922, W. H. Lighty of the Wisconsin extension division polled sixty colleges and universities "that were known or suspected to be interested"[46] in the use of radio for public education purposes. Twenty-four institutions by that time reported radio broadcasting activity, thirteen of which were NUEA member institutions. Fifteen more of the sixty indicated they were "favorably disposed, are considering the matter, or have definite plans underway."[47] While the state colleges and universities led the early broadcasting efforts, such small colleges as Tufts, Antioch, and Marietta were also utilizing the new medium.

Lighty reported that Tufts was a pioneer in the radio broadcasting of faculty lecturers. The broadcasts were made by "station WGI, operated by the American Radio and Research Corporation, situated on Tufts' ground leased from the institution. At present a fifteen-minute lecture once a week is broadcasted."[48] In his survey on the radio activities of other universities, Lighty commented:

> Tulane University, another university not of this [NUEA] affiliation, has broadcasted weekly for approximately one year through its own station operated by the Departments of Electrical Engineering and Physics. The broadcasts have comprised a summary of domestic and foreign trade conditions for the United States Department of Commerce, and lectures and musical programs by members of the university staff, and others invited to participate.
>
> The University of Indiana has broadcasted from a commercial station since last October, two ten-minute addresses once a week. The use of a commercial station has not

proved satisfactory and the present hopes are to establish a
university owned radio station on the campus.

Of the institutions that have been broadcasting through
their own stations, Iowa State College broadcasts daily
weather, market and crop information and occasional educational concerns and athletic contests.[49]

During these first few years of radio development, lectures, recitals, and general interest programs were typically
one-shot presentations. In most cases no effort was made
to coordinate the programs into meaningful series. The
longest such coordinated programming at the University
of Wisconsin, for example, was a series of four consecutive
lectures on agricultural marketing. To Lighty, systematic,
courselike radio instruction was not an immediate concern:

> In my judgement . . . I am persuaded that this kind of
> radio broadcasting may well await further and maturer de-
> velopment. It is more important now to establish in the
> minds of adults everywhere the fact that the modern univer-
> sity holds possibilities for successful, authentic guidance and
> assistance to every citizen capable of reflection.[50]

Lighty further argued that radio would have a positive
effect on the family, unlike other recent inventions which,
in their way, altered American life:

> Radio communication constitutes one of the outstanding
> inventions that is destined to profoundly change our social
> institutions. Compare it with two other outstanding inven-
> tions that have in recent years modified our social life—the
> motion picture film and the automobile. Both of these in-
> ventions have influenced our social life largely away from
> the home or fireside influences. The radio once again but-
> tresses home and family influences. In my boyhood the fire-
> side lure may have been Arabian nights but now for my boy
> it is Radio nights.[51]

While Lighty was discouraging the immediate use of radio for formal extension instruction in Wisconsin, in 1923 a number of other colleges and universities were making plans for just such programming. Pennsylvania State College, for example, used radio lectures to augment correspondence study in the sciences.[52]

While the universities were rapidly moving into the field of radio broadcasting as a means of reaching larger audiences, the mechanics of radio itself became a popular subject of study in both the extension class and by correspondence. The extension division of the Massachusetts Department of Education offered twenty-nine courses with an enrollment of 2,260 in 1925.[53] A similar course offered by the Fort Wayne extension center of Indiana University consisted of ten noncredit lectures offered for a fee of $5. A high school physics teacher, "a very competent man in the radio field,"[54] was recruited when the regular university faculty was unable to find a suitable teacher.

In 1925 the National University Extension Association, recognizing the growing importance of radio, appointed a committee of three persons to report to and "represent the Association in all matters pertaining to broadcasting."[55] During the 1920s the federal government sought to bring order to the rapidly expanding radio industry. At the third in a series of radio broadcasting conferences called by Secretary of Commerce Hoover, the Association of College and University Broadcasting Stations was organized in 1925. The association consisted of thirty-five institutions which sought to secure from the government specific educational wave-lengths "so that they would have their place in the air without the possibility of being overpowered and drowned out by the larger and more powerful commercial stations."[56]

By the end of the 1920s no clear pattern had emerged

from the use of radio for instructional purposes. Some university stations felt compelled to satisfy the wide range of audience interests, offering programs of essentially entertainment value.[57] On the other hand, as B. C. Riley, dean of the University of Florida, general extension division, and director of radio station WRUF, contended:

> . . . entirely too small an audience has been reached by the strictly educational features of the university stations. Too often they are developed by university men who satisfy, in a measure, only that part of the population exacting a type of culture and information which the commercial stations, with their wider appeal, have been compelled to pass. Up to the present time, the educational features of the university state stations have consisted for the most part of sporadic lectures in a few unrelated courses of indefinite appeal. We must add to our educational progress information and cultural features that will interest that legion of adults with little education.[58]

Though no general agreement had been reached on how radio broadcasting could be most satisfactorily integrated into the universities' outreach program, by 1928 Alderman identified sixty-five institutions utilizing radio, including four junior colleges.[59] As the decade came to a close, radio instruction was becoming a general practice with college and university extension divisions. Normally, the broadcasts supplemented the textbook or other reading materials, outlined the main points, and explained different passages.

At the same time, the noneducational motives of university extension, that is, the concern for extending popular and financial support for the institution itself, were apparent as in the earlier development of extension. W. T. Middlebrook, comptroller of the University of Minnesota, acknowledged this public relations use of radio:

Any educational institution which engages in radio broadcasting must be actuated by one or, more likely, by both of these motives—a desire to extend its present off-campus service or a desire to furnish to its constituents, the people of the state in the case of state institutions, information of its activities which will promote a better understanding of its work and further its public support. Either and both motives, in my opinion, justify the existence of an educational station. I do not shun the publicity feature, and I do not undervalue its importance, but I do believe that an extension of its instructional and informational service is the more important.[60]

Between 1923 and 1940 some one hundred forty radio extension courses were broadcast for credit in the United States, the majority of them being offered between 1923 and 1930. During the 1930s it became increasingly difficult for universities to secure radio time from cooperating commercial stations whose operations were no longer experimental but substantial profit-making enterprises. In some cases, regular correspondence courses were revived and replaced radio extension. In addition, the universities by the late 1930s were disillusioned by the ever-increasing expense of operating their own stations even though many had been forced to solicit commercial advertising as a source of revenue.[61] As a result, by 1940, the great enthusiasm for radio shown earlier by extension leaders had largely evaporated.

The Depression and Higher Adult Education

When the great crisis of the 1930s shattered the American economy, institutions of higher education were not long in feeling the effects. Regular student enrollments declined for several years, income from both fees and subsidy fell off, teaching staffs were sharply reduced, and the long-time growth trend of the colleges and universities was, for a time, reversed.[62]

The effect on higher adult education paralleled the general decline of the colleges and universities. Table 5 indicates the magnitude of the decline and the length of its duration.

While the economy started its decline during the last quarter of 1929, it was about two years before the colleges and universities began to suffer serious enrollment losses. This lag was attributed chiefly to the relatively good reserves for those students who were already enrolled in the institutions.[63] Although financial uncertainty undoubtedly prevented many from entering college, for those already enrolled the importance of completing degree programs undoubtedly provided incentive for some students to finish their studies. In addition some state budgets provided appropriations based on the previous year's receipts which further, though temporarily, stabilized the situation.

Few American families escaped the effects of the depression. When the Roosevelt administration took office in 1933, there were millions of young people unable to attend educational institutions or to find employment. The total jobless in that year exceeded 15 million. Among the early legislative acts of the Roosevelt period which affected higher education were the Federal Emergency Relief Administration (FERA) under the guidance of Harry Hopkins, which took relief out of the hands of state and local governments, the Civilian Conservation Corps (CCC) which gave jobs to young men and veterans on relief rolls,[64] and the Works Progress Administration (WPA), established to "organize and coordinate the whole system of public works."[65]

Hundreds of colleges and universities participated in the relief program in a variety of ways. The University of Min-

Table 5.

Higher Adult Education Enrollment in the United States 1919-39*

Year	Resident Enrollment	Extension and Correspondence	Summer Session
1919-20	597,880	101,662	132,849
1921-22	681,076	155,163	220,311
1923-24	823,063	194,147	278,125
1925-26	917,462	324,819	340,461
1927-28	1,053,955	360,246	382,776
1929-30	1,100,737	354,113	388,006
1931-32	1,154,117	440,186	414,260
1933-34	1,055,360	253,991	303,754
1935-36	1,208,227	297,921	370,026
1937-38	1,350,905	371,173	429,864
1939-40	1,494,203	362,381	456,679

*Abstracted from E. J. Foster, *Statistical Summary of Education, 1939-1940,* vol. 2 (Washington, D.C.: Government Printing Office, 1943), p. 30, and Henry G. Badger, Frederick J. Kelly, and Lloyd E. Blauch, *Statistics in Higher Education, 1939-40 and 1941-42,* vol. 2 (Washington, D.C.: Government Printing Office, 1944), p.p. 4, 10.

nesota in 1933 organized its Group Correspondence Study Plan whereby college courses were conducted for high school graduates in local communities throughout the state. Unemployed high school graduates who were unable to go away to college were brought together under "the direction of the local superintendent of schools and Board of Education for group study of courses regularly offered in the freshman year of the university."[66] The local school authorities employed a teacher to supervise the group's progress. If the student later established one year's residence at the university, his credits were transferred to his permanent record.[67]

New York State also established emergency college centers, particularly in the urban areas utilizing "men and women of unusual training and experience who have been forced to apply for relief work."[68] In New York City, hundreds of engineers, architects, artists, musicians, and lawyers were hired to teach classes of unemployed adults. The New York City experiment proved so successful that the program was extended to upstate cities and in a short time employed "between two and three thousand people . . . as teachers and recreation leaders."[69] In addition, relief support allowed orchestras to put on over five hundred concerts in New York City. These programs in New York were sponsored by the New York State Temporary Emergency Relief Administration. The distinction between state-supported programs and federally-supported programs becomes blurred, however, because in some cases federal dollars were distributed through state agencies for welfare and relief activity.

The University of Toledo, in conjunction with a number of other local groups or institutions interested in adult education, organized and operated emergency schools in that city. Philip Nash, president of the university, discussed the program in an address at the 1934 Association of Urban Universities' Conference:

> Last year about 1,400 people registered with us in the emergency school in over 150 classes of college grade taught by 77 well qualified instructors. The whole program was the outgrowth of our Opportunity School where classes were organized for persons who were not able to pay for regular evening college instruction but who wished seriously to study some intellectual interest. The University organized the class, the student received no credit, the instructor got no pay. The emergency school was carried on in a similar

fashion except that those teachers who were entitled to relief help were paid by the CWA [Civil Works Administration] and FERA [Federal Emergency Relief Administration], the others were not paid.

All this was a most interesting experiment, not only for the University but for the other organizations. With our co-operation successful schools were started at several of the churches, at almost all of the community houses, and at the other social agencies.[70]

In addition to these local and regional programs, managed by colleges and universities, the Civilian Conservation Corps had an educational impact on hundreds of thousands of young people and adults. The CCC was described as "a great American folk school"[71] by C. A. Marsh, dean of the University of Buffalo and educational director of the corps:

Let me mention some of the characteristics of the folk school as I see it. It is an educational enterprise for adults and older youths growing out of the native culture of a people who want to learn the things that are of most interest or importance to them. It is not imposed from above, it does not prescribe an individual's curriculum, it meets the immediate needs and interests of the people. In the folk school one group may be studying their social and economic problems, another their vocational problems, another may be satisfying their yearning for self-expression. If you accept this definition . . . , the educational program now going on in the CCC Camps is a great American Folk School. . . .[72]

The camps were organized in the spring of 1933 and operated by the United States Army. By summer 1934 about 370,000 unemployed men were enrolled in the 1,728 camps. About 300,000 were of the eighteen to twenty-five age range and the rest were "War Veterans and experienced woodsmen."[73] By the summer of 1935 some 600,000 men were enrolled including 100,000 veterans and older men.[74] The corps was a product of the ccoperative effort of four government departments, (1) the Labor Department which selected the enrollees, (2) the War Department which built and operated the camps, (3) the Departments of Interior and Agriculture which supervised the daily work of the enrollees, and (4) Interior's Office of Education which conducted the camps' educational program.[75]

Within the educational program, vocational subjects constituted approximately 31 percent of the curriculum, academic subjects 57 percent, and general subjects 12 percent. Marsh commented on the wide range of academic subjects: "To list the subjects that come under the heading of academic courses, one could almost read the combined curricula of the elementary school, the secondary school, and the college. I have even known instances of the teaching of Latin and Chinese."[76]

The extension divisions of many universities played a direct role in the educational program of the CCC. In 1935 Howard W. Oxley of the Office of Education commented on the cooperation of extension units: ". . . it should be said that the university extension division has been the one department of our modern American universities which has been able to adapt its courses most effectively to CCC needs."[77]

Oxley identified correspondence study as the university's great contribution to camp instruction. Correspondence study was made available to corpsmen for a very modest fee, the average rate being $1.50 a credit hour. Instruction ranged from elementary through college and covered both the academic and vocational areas. In the Ninth Corps Area (West Coast) alone, more than eighteen thousand were enrolled in university extension correspondence courses. In some districts as many as 60 percent of the company engaged in correspondence work.[78]

Universities and their extension divisions further made instruction available to the CCC through freshman college centers organized near the camps as well as through extension classes conducted in the camp itself. The centers were funded by the National Youth Administration. Five colleges and universities in Texas alone established centers for the CCC as Oxley reported:

> These Centers are under the general supervision of the five universities . . . , teachers are drawn from the NYA student-aid rolls; and CCC enrollees are extended advanced training free of charge. One hundred and thirty-two CCC enrollees are pursuing college work through this plan. Work done by enrollees in each of these centers is accredited by the sponsoring institution and has the value in terms of credits, of work done in the institution itself.[79]

The universities also encouraged members of their faculties to give lectures at the camps. These talks brought information to corpsmen on such subjects as job-interviewing, citizenship, travel, science, and current events. In several states, it was reported, extension lecturers brought visual aids, including lantern slides, to enhance their talks.[80]

There were other ways, as well, in which the universities aided the instructional program of the CCC. Summer conferences for CCC advisers were held on university campuses and in some cases academic credit was extended to participants. Throughout the year, college faculty aided corps officials "in the preparation of special courses and reading lists for Camp Advisers."[81] In some cases, when a camp was located near the campus, CCC enrollees were allowed to use the institution's facilities, including the library, classrooms, laboratories, gymnasium, and athletic field. A number of colleges donated books to the libraries of nearby CCC camps, and the Universities of Virginia and Michigan sent art and forestry exhibits into the camps of their states. Several universities offered scholarships and other financial aid to corpsmen. The University of Wisconsin offered $20,000 in CCC scholarships for its correspondence program.[82]

In all, the universities supported the work of the CCC to a remarkable degree. The relationship between institutions of higher education and the corps was a model of cooperation. The great crisis which brought about that cooperation was of a magnitude without precedent in American history, though it would only be a few short years before external circumstances would again force the government and the educational establishment into intensely coordinated activity.

As the 1930s came to a close the formation of the Association of Urban Evening Colleges attested to the continuing differentiation of adult education activities and resulting professional organizations. Some years earlier, in 1926, at the urging of the Carnegie Corporation, the American Association for Adult Education (AAAE) held the first of what would be annual meetings in Chicago. A Carnegie advisory committee had commented one year earlier:

> There is no phase of current educational development that is making more rapid and significant strides than adult education. It is full of vitality and promise but it is sporadic and experimental. . . . Though many national bodies deal with the different parts of the field, there is no agency that concerns itself with the problem of adult education as a whole. That such an organization, cooperative and advisory in character, could give impetus, solidity and drive to all parts of the movement, is beyond question.[83]

By the late 1920s there had existed some four hundred organizations dealing with problems of adult education. The AAAE continued its role as the leading national coordinating body for adult education in the United States until 1941, when its supporter, the Carnegie Corporation, concluded its resources would be more appropriately used for the promotion of institutions directly training leaders in adult education.

As reported earlier, the Association of Urban Universities from its inception in 1914 had exhibited great concern for the development of higher adult education, with evening college deans as often as not outnumbering day administrators at the annual conferences. In 1939, however, the association's leaders decided to invite presidents rather than evening deans to represent their institutions at the meetings. The result was the formation of the Association of Urban Evening Colleges under the leadership of evening college deans. Dyer reported that:

> Although the evening college group may have been a bit piqued, actually there seems to have been little bitterness engendered over the break. For several years the two groups met concurrently and then drifted away from each other by selecting separate meeting places and times. . . . The separation could also be taken as a tacit recognition of the fact that evening college education was attaining a personality of its own.[84]

By 1940 the back of the depression had been broken, and enrollments in the various evening colleges and extension programs had recovered, approaching or surpassing the highs achieved during the late 1920s and early 1930s. With economic life returning to a more stable pattern, educational institutions, too, seemed about to return to a steady period of growth. However, World War II and its aftermath would to a great degree disrupt the expected development.

World War II and the Universities

The crisis placed special demands on institutions of higher education. Within a short period of time, colleges and universities were involved directly in the training of the fighting force, including flight personnel as well as those involved in a vast array of war support areas. Most important, perhaps, was the training of engineers and other specialized personnel. For this task the federal government established the Engineering, Science, and Management War Training Program (ESMWT), an operation which lasted five years. The program was financed through the United States Office of Education and was instructed to "assist private industry with war contracts in selecting, recruiting, and training the additional manpower needed for all-out war production."[85] Many cooperating universities operated the programs through their extension divisions. By 1945 a total of 1,795,716 trainees had gone through the ESMWT programs, 34 percent through eight large extension divisions alone.[86]

A substantial correspondence program was organized in 1941 by the United States Army Institute, later called the United States Armed Forces Institute. The first chief of USAFI was W. R. Young, the director of correspondence instruction at Pennsylvania State University. Most of the NUEA member institutions participated in instructing servicemen and the operation long outlasted the war itself.[87] The government paid one-half the costs of the texts and tuition fees not to exceed $20 for any one course. At the request of the War Department, the institute's correspondence courses were offered to enemy prisoners of war in this country, and, through the War Prisoners' Aid of the YMCA, American prisoners in Germany also had access to the program.[88]

The universities were involved in a host of other war-directed activities, including conferences, institutes, and information centers. The civilian morale branch of the government, under the direction of New York Mayor La Guardia, sought to enlighten the population on questions of war, democracy, and citizenship. Universities were involved in organizing forums, contests, library exhibits, and teaching classes in English, history, and citizenship.[89]

The war experience called for a major readjustment for the universities and their extension divisions:

> The war ... had great significance for university extension. Resident faculty members lacking students on campus were employed off campus, when qualified, to teach adults in centers under unusual time schedules. Academic departments were required to develop courses of instruction for these programs. Colleges developed new relationships with industry and government [extension directors served on many national committees]. Industry discovered that colleges could give practical intensive training courses urgently needed to meet emergency needs. . . ."[90]

The war effort greatly expanded the normal scope of extension programs. In part, the emergency situation provided the universities with an experience and training they would need when returning veterans made additional demands on their educational facilities at the war's conclusion. While the problems of the late 1940s and early 1950s did not precisely parallel those which came out of the international crisis, that experience served to broaden the universities and established, in a substantial way, the universities' affiliation with the federal government.

6

The Modern Era

The most striking feature of American higher education during the latter half of the 1940s and early 1950s was the assimilation of millions of World War II veterans. Perhaps, as Shannon and Schoenfeld commented, "The flood of veterans to the campus in 1946–47 was merely symptomatic of a broad American thirst for knowledge and a deep national conviction that knowledge was power."[1] A more powerful personal motive was also at work, namely, the realiatzion that training and education opened the door of opportunity in modern America.

The war had postponed or interrupted the education of millions of American men and women between 1941 and 1945. The federal government before the end of the war was concerned with the reorientation of the soldier to civilian status. The Veterans Administration (VA) was charged with the direction and coordination of a variety of services. In addition to education and vocational rehabilitation, they included programs of compensation, pensions, loan guarantees, life insurance, death benefits, and medical care.[2]

The GI Bills

The basic acts which related to education and vocational rehabilitation were: (1) Public Law 16 and (2) Public Law 346 of the Servicemen's Readjustment Act of 1944. The VA was authorized by Public Law 16 to prescribe, provide, and supervise a program of vocational rehabilitation for disabled World War II veterans.[3] The purpose of the program was "to restore employability lost by virtue of a handicap due to service-incurred disability,"[4] and it covered every phase of the rehabilitation process from "the veteran's initial application through various courses in educational preparation, and provide[d] assistance for his placement in suitable employment."[5]

The colleges and universities were more directly concerned with Public Law 346 through which the Veterans Administration provided "a program of education and training which [made] it possible for an eligible veteran to pursue a course of his own choice in any approved school or job-training establishment which [would] accept him."[6] To be eligible under the original act, the veteran had to initiate his program before 25 July 1951, or within four years of his discharge from the service, whichever came later. Subsequent bills were eventually passed by Congress to allow men with more recent military service to attend college on the government subsidy.[7]

By June 1951 a total of 16,000 approved educational institutions, including schools, colleges, and vocational institutes, had enrolled veterans. The VA had contracted with the various schools for the payment of tuition, fees, books, and equipment expenses incurred by the supported student. President Truman, in his budget message delivered on 2 January 1951, commented on the veterans' education program:

> Expenditures for education and training of World War II veterans are estimated at 625 million dollars in the fiscal year 1953, a decline of 860 million dollars from the revised estimates for the current fiscal year. The 1953 expenditures will provide for an average enrollment of 491,000 in school, job, and farm training courses. The reduction from an average enrollment of over one million in the current fiscal year reflects the fact that July 25, 1951, was the deadline for initiation of training under the program. By the end of the fiscal year 1953, approximately 7,800,000 veterans— about half of all the veterans of World War II—will have received education and training at a cost to the Government of 14.3 billion dollars. This investment is already proving to be of great benefit to the veterans and the nation.[8]

The degree to which colleges and universities were involved in the original GI bill programs is indicated in Table 6:

Table 6.

Average Number of Veterans Enrolled in
Higher Educational Programs Offered by the Veterans
Administration in the 5 Months from October
through March, 1945-46 to 1950-51*

Year	Number of Veterans
1945-46	209,313
1946-47	1,095,975
1947-48	1,180,350
1948-49	1,024,924
1949-50	851,290
1950-51	558,523

*Statistics abstracted from Table 41, Hutchins and Munse, *Federal Funds for Education, 1950-51 and 1951-52*, p. 73.

The figures offered in Table 6 take on added meaning when it is recalled that at the program's peak in the 1947 academic year, one out of every two college students was a veteran. Moreover, three out of every four male students were veterans.[9] In all, of the nearly eleven million veterans of World War II and Korea who entered an educational or training program, approximately three and one-half million attended institutions of higher education. Of particular interest was the fact that while about 30 percent of the eligible World War II veterans took advantage of the GI bill and attended college, about 50 percent of the eligible Korean veterans did so.[10]

Although accounting for this remarkable increase cannot be done with certainty, four factors seem likely to have influenced that trend. First, the increasing importance of a college education for social and economic mobility was keenly felt during this period. Second, the economy was generally healthy, and the young adult was somewhat less likely to be needed at home by his parents. Third, higher education was increasingly accessible, particularly due to the proliferation of public junior colleges. And finally, the original GI bill had been widely publicized and the veteran of the Korean War was less hesitant to enter a college program than his World War II counterpart had been.

The colleges and universities were ill equipped to handle the great increase in enrollments after World War II. In order to accommodate millions of additional students two developments occurred which paved the way for the veteran-student. The Surplus Property Act of 1944 and subsequent legislation provided "many millions of dollars' worth of real and personal property [which] were donated or sold at large discounts to colleges and universities."[11] In addition to land and buildings, the wide range of other surplus materials included aircraft, laboratory equipment, electronic gear, machine tools, maintenance supplies, office machines, and vehicles of all types.[12]

Higher educational institutions benefited as well from the College Housing Act of 1950 which enabled colleges and universities "to obtain from the Federal Government long-term loans at low-interest rates for the construction of student and faculty housing."[13] From the beginning of the housing program in 1950 through June 1956, three hundred and twenty loans had been made for a total of $221 million and additional loans of nearly that magnitude were pending.[14]

The influx of veterans had an impact on the regular day programs in higher education. Studies of several institutions indicated veterans did as well as or better than nonveterans as measured by grade point averages.[15] An article in *Life* described somewhat impressionistically Harvard's reaction (and perhaps the reporter's reaction) to the veteran-students:

"The window gazers and the hibernators have vanished," says one professor. "This crowd never takes its eyes off you," says another. A third says, "You've got to be awfully careful. These kids have been everywhere; they have stored up an enormous amount of information." A fourth finds, "Sure, there are plenty of radicals but there's not much ideology. These men don't want to tear everything down; they want to make the existing system work better." And Provost Buck, who has been on the faculty for 20 years, has decided, "There is a strong strain of idealism in these young men. They want to do a good job."[16]

The continuing education divisions, the evening colleges, the extension centers, and the correspondence programs were also deeply affected by the new wave of students. In November 1951, ten thousand veterans were enrolled in correspondence study programs alone from eighty-nine institutions of higher learning.[17]

Military Extension Programs

Three institutions (the University of Maryland, the University of California, and Louisiana State University) initiated overseas extension training programs in Europe, the Far East, and in the Caribbean. In 1950 the University of California opened its classes in Japan and maintained them despite the outbreak of the Korean War. Louisiana State Centers were opened in the Caribbean, taught by regular university faculty, and students' records were filed with those kept for on-campus students at Baton Rouge.[18] These centers were the result of a 1947 army directive which was issued to encourage officers to improve their education and which prescribed that "the immediate goal in this educational improvement would be to raise all Regular Army Officers to two years of college, with an ultimate objective of a baccalaureate degree."[19]

The most ambitious overseas extension program was conducted by the University of Maryland. The Maryland Board of Regents in 1947 created the College of Special and Continuation Studies. Originally the CSCS, as the college came to be known, was organized to provide higher education for adults within Maryland. In a short time, however, it became apparent that the new college could also be of service to military personnel stationed at Fort Meade, at the Pentagon, at Aberdeen Proving Ground, and at Bolling and Andrews Air Force Bases.[20] By 1957 these off-campus programs were enrolling more than one thousand students alone in classes at the Pentagon.

Through the administrative experience gained initially in these military surroundings, the CSCS was prepared when

"Armed Forces officials invited American Universities to submit proposals for offering courses to servicemen stationed in Europe."[21] In the fall of 1949, expecting to teach about five hundred students, a few instructors were flown from Maryland to Germany. When eighteen hundred students enrolled, it became apparent that additional space, teachers, and books were needed, and Ray Ehrenberger, later dean of CSCS, was dispatched to Germany to resolve the problems which arose.

From this modest beginning grew the three divisions of the Maryland Overseas Program: the European, the North Atlantic, and the Far East Divisions. The European Division was headquartered in Heidelberg, Germany, and offered courses on the Continent, in the United Kingdom, North Africa, and the Middle East. In 1949 qualified sons and daughters of government personnel were permitted to enroll in the CSCS program at the freshman and sophomore levels. In 1951, the North Atlantic Division was organized and classes were offered in Newfoundland, Labrador, Greenland, and Iceland. The last of the three, the Far East Division, was established in 1956 and offered courses to servicemen in Japan, Korea, and Okinawa.[22]

In all, over two hundred teaching centers located on military installations abroad were operated by the University of Maryland. In 1956 some fifteen thousand students took courses in the liberal arts, business administration, and speech. Who were these students taking courses overseas?

> ... they are mechanics, pilots, navigators, radar operators, instructors, and practitioners of a thousand other specialties. They work in sections concerned with supply, maintenance, intelligence, transportation, public relations, plans and operations and many other activities. They attend Maryland classes off-duty: they meet two evenings a week, three hours each meeting, for eight weeks receiving residence (not extension) credit in the amount of three semester hours.

> Most of the students transfer their accumulated overseas
> course credits to home universities. . . . One study of nearly
> four hundred former Overseas Program students . . . showed
> that one hundred and ten of them had already won degrees
> at eighty-three different institutions, twenty-two earning de-
> grees "with distinction."[23]

The responsibility for recommending overseas program
faculty was left to the individual department heads at the
College Park Campus. In addition to considering the academic qualifications of a prospective teacher, it was reported
that serious attention was given "to the applicant's ability
to conduct himself with credit while he is far removed from
his department head and dean."[24]

Professor Loren Reid, who taught speech in the overseas
program during the 1952–53 year as well as special courses
in 1955, commented enthusiastically, if with some bias:

> I call the Overseas Program the educational phenomenon
> of this age. As an imaginative concept I rank it ahead of the
> founding of the American summer school and the American
> Junior College. The summer school found a new time for
> education, the summer months; the junior college found a
> new space, the large towns and cities; the Overseas Program
> found both. It found a new time previously overlooked, the
> period of military service; and it found new space, on the
> bases of overseas military installations.[25]

The overseas programs of the several universities which
undertook them were, indeed, imaginative. They represented a marked deviation of the traditional practice of
American institutions of higher education. While these programs reached far fewer servicemen than the resident campus programs did through the GI bill, they nonetheless
were forged without precedent and deserve recognition on
that basis.

Residential Conference Centers

During the 1940s and 1950s, while the universities were accepting responsibility for the higher education of active military personnel and veterans, both on and off campus, another development, though less spectacular, drew considerable attention. The conference center, a separate university building, often equipped to house and board, and used for adult conferences and short courses, appeared in great numbers particularly by the 1960s. Although Harold J. Alford, in his study of the Kellogg residential centers, identified two early centers, one of which dated back to the 1880s,[26] the modern conference center is generally traced to the University of Minnesota's Center for Continuation Study, established in 1936.

The Minnesota Center was built during the depression and funded by the Public Works Administration. The center was conceived by Minnesota's President Lotus D. Coffman and was "the first specially designed campus facility for residential continuing education."[27] The first director of the center, Harold Benjamin, had been associated for years with several Danish-American folk high schools. The legendary folk high school in Denmark had been the prototype institution for those established by Danish-Americans who had settled in America. During the early 1930s, when President Coffman first proposed building a center for adult education on the university's campus, he acknowledged the Danish influence: "the so-called adult education movement will gradually take form . . . somewhat similar to that which is provided in the Folk-Schule of Denmark."[28]

In 1937 Benjamin was invited by the National University Extension Association to address that organization on the subject of the Minnesota Center. Benjamin recalled that, at the ceremonial opening of the center, there were a variety of opinions concerning the scope of the new institution and that frequent reference "was made to the fact that there were many alternative uses to which the building and equipment could be put, if, and when, the experiment should fail."[29]

The Minnesota Center consisted of dining rooms, lobbies, a lounge, sitting rooms, conference rooms, a chapel, bedrooms, and double offices for the director and the housing manager. The facility "gave ample instructional and living quarters for a maximum of one hundred twenty students."[30]

During its first year of operation, 1936–37, the center held eighteen institutes. Of these, two were four weeks in length, six were one week long, and the others were of shorter duration. In his address to the NUEA, Benjamin commented on the total instructional environment the center hoped to achieve:

> No matter whether the time for a particular institute is long or short ... the center becomes the exclusive residential college for that institute during its term. All instructional work with the exception of clinics, laboratory projects, excursions, and some of the reference work which has to be carried on in the general library of the university is conducted in the building. The lounge and dining room are also considered fundamental instruments for carrying on the work of an institute.[31]

The institutes offered at the center ranged from courses for "strictly professional ... through semi-professional, occupational, mixed occupational and vocational, and civic groups to courses of a general cultural nature."[32] Teachers, hospital administrators, pharmacists, probation and parole officers, photographers, and waterworks' managers were among those who used the facility during its first year.

The Minnesota Center clearly demonstrated the utility of residential higher adult education, but it was the W. K. Kellogg Foundation's interest in similar projects that actually stimulated the great proliferation of conference centers.

The foundation bearing the Battle Creek cereal manufacturer's name had long been involved in educational work in Michigan. Since 1938 it had supported the Farm Youth Institute, a short-course program offered by Michigan State College (later University) to its rural constituency. Alford reported, "The institute had been very successful, and John A. Hannah, president of the college, wanted not only to continue it but also to expand it."[33]

In addition to the Farm Youth Program, the Kellogg Foundation had also been active in supporting adult health, education, welfare, and recreation in the seven-county rural area around Battle Creek. The program was known as the Michigan Community Health Project.[34]

During the early 1940s, when the foundation was hopeful of phasing out of the successful Farm Youth Institute, anticipating further support of adult education activity, President Hannah proposed during the early 1940s the development of an adult rural life institute. By 1945 the long-time Michigan State president had more clearly defined his scheme:

> I have a notion that we might kill two or three birds with one stone by tying together a building project devoted to continuing education, with classrooms and facilities for handling the conferences and very short courses, providing housing and feeding facilities, and at the same time providing facilities for teaching courses in hotel administration.[35]

As a result of conversations between Hannah, the Kellogg Foundation, and the hotel association, in September of 1945 the foundation board of trustees authorized $1 million for the construction of the center. After "much planning and many frustrations and changes," the Kellogg Center at Michigan State University was opened on 23 September 1951.

By this time, the on- or off-campus conference center was not altogether unknown to adult educators. During the 1940s and 1950s other institutions had been recipients of lodges and estates which were well suited for adult programs.

By 1951, when the Michigan State center opened, the NUEA was already developing "Criteria for university sponsorship of trade and professional institutes . . . and procedures in setting [them] up. . . ."[36] At an NUEA conference and institute symposium the following year, Merle McClure of Purdue University proposed five guidelines for the university's residential program:

(1) The public should be the ultimate beneficiary of each activity.

(2) The university should use as many members of the faculty as appropriate or possible in each conference or institute.

(3) Each conference or institute should have substantial educational content.

(4) Conferences and institutes should not be isolated from campus life, and should include a broad range of university resources including libraries, laboratories, media, and so on.

(5) Leadership in planning conferences and institutes should be the responsibility of the university's extension division.[37]

Extension leaders were aware of the pitfalls inherent in opening the conference center to community and professional groups and organizations. "Rather than to become fully occupied with activities on the periphery," Robert Brown remarked, "we must adhere to our central functions of the college level."[38] This view of maintaining the college level in conference programming was not shared by all, however. Maurice Chaffu argued: "Needs and requests for programs that are in the public interest should receive priority. . . . We should strive to help all people on all achievement levels—from the lower up through the graduate level—for this is one of the aims of adult education."[39]

This question of how much and what type of adult education is appropriate for a university to carry on has been, and will likely continue to be, a perplexing problem for institutions of higher learning. The question is not limited to the conference center. It is one which every university continuing education administrator must constantly face and ultimately settle within his own institution's financial, philosophical, and human resource limitations. Perhaps nowhere on the university campus is the problem of purpose and priority more sensitive or difficult to resolve than in the continuing education division.

The adult education center at Michigan State was only the first of many such facilities supported by the Kellogg Foundation between 1945 and 1970. During the 1950s and 1960s the foundation helped finance continuing education centers at the universities of Nebraska, Oklahoma, Chicago, Oxford (England), Notre Dame, Columbia (New York), Georgia, and, in 1966, the foundation joined a consortium of six universities to develop the New England Center.

The New England Center was probably the most imaginative continuing education facility in the country. By 1966, when the Kellogg Foundation had plans to phase out the support of such centers, six New England state universities proposed an altogether new idea for residential higher adult education. A single center, located near the University of New Hampshire campus but to serve and be supported by six states, was the central idea of the plan. In this regional effort, each university concentrated on specific problem areas:

> Maine, to stimulate cooperative approaches to the development, conservation and effective use of New England's economic, natural and human resources;
> New Hampshire, to design an interdisciplinary interinstitutional graduate program in adult education;
> Vermont, to develop programs in continuing medical education;
> Massachusetts, to enhance student culture and develop community colleges;
> Connecticut, to develop continuing education programs in the visual and performing arts; and
> Rhode Island, to concentrate upon education for and service to the aging.[40]

The rapid growth of residential conference centers across the country provided a means whereby the practice and process of adult education could be systematically studied. The centers, in addition to their primary function, became laboratories in adult learning. In 1965, the Studies and Training Program in Continuing Education at the University of Chicago, with support of the Kellogg Foundation, began publication of the *Continuing Education Report,* a periodical to "summarize various investigations and to express viewpoints, sometimes controversial, concerning the proper role of this new field of university endeavor."[41]

During the 1960s, the conference or institute, the fastest growing segment of university extension since World War II,[42] became the subject of intense analysis. Donald Deppe reported that conference directors were of five types: (1) client-oriented, (2) operations-oriented, (3) image-oriented, (4) institution-oriented, and (5) problem-oriented,[43] and he concluded "the majority . . . will make beneficial contributions to this relatively new and increasingly significant area of higher Adult Education."[44] Devlin and Litchfield, reporting on ten centers, determined that the number of conference participants ranged from less than fifty to over five hundred, that nearly two-thirds of the conferences were three days or less in length,[45] and that 80 percent of the conferences "were dominated by programs with occupational purposes based on professional and technical content."[46]

The conference center, then, was no longer a single-purpose facility. In theory, at least, in addition to the instructional function for which it was designed, the center could also serve as a "site of research into the nature of adult education itself," as well as to "furnish an important means for the education of the leaders of the adult educational movement itself."[47] Whether such functions were performed by more than a few of the seventy-nine conference centers identified by Alford in 1968[48] is unclear.

Educational Television

The period after World War II saw the spectacular rise of a new popular communications medium. As with radio, three decades earlier, many educators believed instruction through television would reshape American society by reaching millions in a way never before possible.

At the end of the war, the Federal Communications Commission reserved thirteen channels in the Very High Frequency Band (VHF) for television broadcasting. When channel one was eliminated, it was thought 394 individual station assignments were possible. Because of interference, however, in 1948 the FCC issued a freeze limiting the number of television stations in the United States to 108.

Unlike the "apathy and short-sightedness which . . . characterized their attitude in the early days of radio,"[49] the National Association of Educational Broadcasters worked hard for the reservation of channels to be used for educational purposes. Three factors were cited for the aggressive stance taken by interested educators:

(1) They recognized that television had a much greater potential for education than did radio and therefore wanted to be sure of a chance for its use;
(2) they were disappointed with their record in radio and did not want to repeat the same mistake in television; and
(3) they had often been dissatisfied with commercial radio's attitude toward education and public service programming and therefore did not want to be entirely dependent upon the industry for educational television programming.[50]

In the end, although channels were reserved for educational purposes, both commercial and educational stations were involved in instructional programming. The commercial stations, in fact, preceded the educational stations in instructional programming, and until the early 1950s all stations in the United States were profit-making corporations. Both network service and instructional broadcasting began on commercial stations about 1948.[51] By 1953 it was reported 136 colleges and universities were offering television courses, with half of the institutions granting credit for successful completion.[52]

Station WOI–TV began operations on 21 February 1950 as the first station on a college or university campus. From its studios at the State College of Iowa at Ames, the station "broadcast[ed] for schools each afternoon and for general audiences each evening Monday through Friday . . . serving an area fifty-five miles in radius . . . and a population . . . of 600,000 people."[53] The pioneer station's programming reflected that of its sister radio station (WOI) serving the "special and general interests of Iowa farmers and homemakers, schools, and adult education groups, as well as the general public."[54] WOI–TV's programs included operatic productions, drama, popular science, and world affairs.

During the 1950s and 1960s hundreds of other colleges and universities utilized television in one way or another. In some cases, the universities produced cultural programs which were broadcast by nearby commercial stations. Other institutions created formal courses and contracted with commercial stations to reach an audience. In a few instances credit courses were developed by universities and given national exposure. Johns Hopkins created "Science Review," which enjoyed a thirteen-year run on a national network.

Perhaps the two best-known instructional series presented on commercial television were "Continental Classroom" (NBC) and "Sunrise Semester" (CBS). The courses over the years attracted large audiences and were taken for credit by many people in spite of the fact that locally-affiliated stations frequently offered them at inconvenient hours of the day.[55] In addition many universities produced single programs, particularly in the creative arts, which were broadcast by educational stations.

Philip Lewis estimated that one hundred and seventeen colleges and universities were using television for formal instruction in 1961. These institutions either bought air time from the commercial station or offered the instructional material to the station at no charge to be broadcast as a public service.[56]

By the late 1960s much of the original enthusiasm for university instructional television had waned, although there are today those who see in public television, cable television, and cassette television, instructional opportunities which radio and over-the-air television left unfulfilled. The expectation expressed in 1953 that educational television would have an impact on commercial television, pro-

vide "a real competition . . . and in the long run . . . raise
the level of quality of all television,"[57] was largely wishful
thinking. There had been no precedent for such an outcome
for radio had chiefly been reduced to mass-appeal, entertainment programming; and during the 1950s and 1960s,
this would be the fate of television as well.

Community Development

The period since the end of World War II witnessed a
growing interest in community problems by practitioners
of adult education and others. It was becoming increasingly
apparent that no two communities were alike, and as they
differed, their problems and needs called for individual and
unique methods of study and resolution. Adult educators
reasoned that "recognition of a community of its needs
leads to community organizations,"[58] and during this period a great number of local adult education councils
emerged. Extension leaders were early urged not to become
too involved: "We can assist but we must let the community recognize and do. What we need is fingertip sensitivity
when we work with community groups. . . ."[59]

In 1955 the NUEA formally created its Division of
Community Development and set about undertaking "an
informal survey of the scope and status of community development programs in extension."[60] Three years later, at
the Salt Lake City Conference, Richard W. Poston suggested that the ultimate goal of community development
was to help create through a process of "organized study,
planning, and action . . . a physical and social environment
that is best suited to the maximum growth, development
and happiness of human beings as individuals and as productive members of their society."[61]

The association's Division of Community Development

worked to define the role of the university in community development, and in 1960 the following parameters were proposed:

(1) Basically the community development function aims to help citizens help themselves in solving community problems, through democratic processes.

(2) The community development function involves the process by which the efforts of the people themselves are united with those of other institutions, authorities, and agencies of a public character to improve the economic, social and cultural conditions of communities.

(3) Occupying neutral ground, the impartial university is in a position to assist and guide groups and individuals in working together for solutions to their problems. It is a catalytic agent.

(4) It can bring to bear the knowledge of many academic disciplines involved in the community development process. It is a repository of knowledge.

(5) When it alone cannot provide the required knowledge, the university can identify and make available sources of knowledge from other institutions, authorities, and agencies. It is a clearinghouse of knowledge.[62]

Throughout the country, often by means of their extension divisions, universities began working with community groups and leaders, often without fanfare or publicity, and in spite of the fact that there was "no universal agreement among administrators as to how a community development [program] should be established."[63]

For many years the University of Michigan had operated a program in community-adult education under the direction of the school of education and the extension service. The department concerned itself chiefly with the acquisition of knowledge about community affairs and problems, in addition to the development of a program for the training of professional community workers.

A chief outcome was the emergence of an area confer-

ence for community self-help. The conference was intended
to serve "as a means for initiating a diagnostic look at community affairs, and [to create] a new readiness on the part
of responsible citizens for attacking the solution of local
problems."[64] The conferences also aimed to encourage
self-surveys, discussions courses, citizens' committees, and
community councils to aid the local community in developing the machinery and capacity of looking at itself as a
whole.

During the early 1960s the University of West Virginia
organized the West Virginia Appalachian Center to serve
an eight-county area as a unit. Five of the counties were declining in population, reducing public services, and the
economy was considered stagnant. Because the communities within these counties had no method of dealing with the
deteriorating situation, the Appalachian center, with its
expertise, sought to "facilitate a joint effort involving community residents, government, business, colleges, universities, public and private school systems, and all the other
major interests in the area."[65] As a coordinating agency,
the center worked to renew the eight-county area, both
economically and culturally.

The community development programs which colleges
and universities embarked upon during the 1950s and
1960s had two essentially distinct purposes: the first was
the training of local leaders to better understand the problems of their communities and the second was the preparation of professional field workers, who, as a result of
systematic study in a variety of disciplines, could aid the
community in its self-help effort. Community development,
in a sense, was a recognition that change had occurred and,
local development not keeping pace, had resulted in a de-
terioration of the social and economic condition of the
community. Significantly community development did not
occur when communities prospered; it emerged only after

problems surfaced. Looking back over the last twenty years, one could hardly speak of the success of community development, nor could one attack its failures. The inequities and problems which communities early faced are recognized today as being extremely complex. The community problems were, in fact, reflective of great social and economic problems deeply ingrained in American society. Community development workers, for all their efforts, were not in a position to right the underlying inequities which are so apparent and confront America in the 1970s.

Special University Programs for Adults

While the universities were responding to social problems through community development, new areas of programming in higher adult education were emerging as well. The trend toward special programming designed for adults was in part due to the continued development of professional organizations and associations concerned with adult education.

In 1951, the AAAE, which had been supported by the Carnegie Corporation, and the NEA Department of Adult Education voted to dissolve their organizations and formed the Adult Education Association. During the ensuing years, the AEA was to enjoy the sponsorship of the (Ford Foundation) Fund for Adult Education. In addition to general activity support, the fund subsidized publication of the journal *Adult Leadership*.

The same year in which AEA was founded, the Center for the Study of Liberal Education for Adults appeared. The CSLEA was formed as a result of a proposal made by an AUEC Committee on Liberal Education to the Fund for Adult Education. The fund agreed to support CSLEA, and for seventeen years the organization studied and published monographs on university programs of liberal education for adults, as well as methods of teaching liberal adult education. These organizations, and especially the CSLEA, carefully studied the adult learner and as a result, by the late 1950s, degree and nondegree programs designed for adults were offered with increasing frequency.

Many universities began offering programs specifically for women "who, after years of being homebound while raising their children, [were] again interested in activity outside and apart from the home."[66] Some of the programs were directed to problems of home and family, others dealt with the training and readjustment to a life of employment. A number of schools, the University of Minnesota, Sarah Lawrence, Simmons College, and Syracuse University, "in addition to . . . courses and seminars, placed a special emphasis on counseling to assist women to determine the kind of work and study they would like to engage in."[67] Other efforts were directed to help women formulate and undertake their own continuing programs of education with no goal beyond personal growth and satisfaction.

At Queens College, adult seminars were developed which emphasized "the notion that a course for adults not only can start them where they are, but can be flexible enough to allow cooperation of both students and teacher in reshaping its content and method."[68] The Queens program utilized experience, both past experiences and new experiences selected from the vast resources of the city: its museums, galleries, theaters, newspapers, political structure, people, and so on. The experiences were then reported and discussed in group sessions on the campus.[69] It was reported that not only would the courses be "organized and taught with due consideration for adult characteristics, but the program as a whole will be arranged to fit the daily lives of adults."[70]

During the late 1950s and 1960s art and cultural programs were offered with greater frequency, serving the rapidly expanding cultural interests and needs of the community. Liveright and Goldman reported that colleges and universities in remote areas as well as urban institutions were becoming centers for artistic and cultural life.[71] For the most part these activities have been offered "by the internal university art divisions rather than by adult departments, but almost always adults are involved as audience."[72] Increasingly colleges and universities were building concert halls, supporting regional theaters, promoting summer art festivals, and organizing film societies. In addition, evening colleges often created workshops and courses in art and art appreciation which drew heavily from the community.

A number of schools had begun offering courses specifically designed for older people. During the 1950s St. Louis University was one of the first schools to develop a curriculum in this area. Courses were developed along two lines:

> Classes for senior citizens include *Preparation for Retirement* (for personnel men) and *Preparation for Retirement* (for persons 35 to 60 years of age). Thus, through these two courses the University serves persons who are responsible for industrial or business retirement programs and, in the second case, serves adults directly. In a lecture course for personnel men, the subjects considered are problems of the aged, physical health, mental hygiene, financial preparation for retirement, education for continuing usefulness—alternatives to retirement and how to retrain—and aging employees and their problems. . . .[73]

In addition, St. Louis offered courses to encourage hobbies and part-time employment after sixty, as well as a course directed to community leaders who were responsible for implementing programs for the aged.

By 1963, at least seven institutions were offering degree

programs designed especially for adults.[74] The Bachelor of Liberal Studies Program at the University of Oklahoma came out of a series of faculty-administration seminars during the year 1957–58. After three years of planning and funded by a grant from the Carnegie Corporation, a degree program based on the following objectives emerged:

(1) Knowledge of the natural sciences, social sciences, and humanities in such depth so as to enable the student to understand the relation between the three broad areas, and as well as the research method and works of scholars;

(2) Understanding one's self;

(3) Understanding the behavior of individuals and groups and cultures;

(4) A historical view of man's development;

(5) and an understanding of great literary, scientific, and artistic works.[75]

The B.L.S. program promoted independent study reading from a list of 120 basic books as directed by an adviser. In addition, the student took part in discussion groups on and off campus, participated in "weekend residentials at the Oklahoma Center, audited either regular or evening college courses, engaged in correspondence study, and utilized educational radio and television."[76]

Goddard College, a small, private institution in Vermont, was somewhat unique in that it required adults participating in its special program to be at least twenty-six years old and have been out of college for at least five years. In addition students were required to have completed at least one year of successful college work. The Goddard plan called for a great deal of independent study (for periods of six months) and week-long seminars at the college between the periods of independent study. The student's individually tailored program encouraged student-faculty contact through correspondence, telephone conversations, the exchange of tape recordings, a monthly newsletter with progress reports on students' work, regional group meetings with faculty, as well as short visits to the campus.[77]

Such programs as described at Queens, St. Louis, Oklahoma, and Goddard were highly innovative when they were first introduced. Today, however, no single study could adequately detail the variety of programs specifically designed for adults.

These special adult programs have not been limited to single residential institutions. Inspired in part by England's open university, which has incorporated a host of nontraditional methods of teaching in offering "part-time students twenty-one years of age and older the opportunity to work for bachelor of arts degrees,"[78] as well as by the Goddard adult program and Antioch's off-campus experience program, the State University of New York, in 1971, began formulating plans for an Empire State College. Students at the new college would "earn degrees without being attached to a specific campus, or having to enroll in traditional courses. . . ."[79]

Operation of the college began in the Albany and Rochester areas and regional learning centers extended throughout the state by 1978. The goal of the nonresidential institution is to broaden educational options for people of all ages who have graduated from high school but who, for one reason or another, cannot or prefer not to secure a higher education in the traditional manner.

An Empire State College coordinating center is located on the old campus of Skidmore College in Saratoga Springs; plans call for eventually some twenty learning centers scattered about the state. Through these regional learning centers the student will "apply for admission, formulate his program with a faculty adviser, periodically receive educational material and counseling and possibly arrange for some instruction by tutors at or away from the center."[80]

The college grants academic credit for correspondence

study as well as "education courses on television, on-the-job and community volunteer experiences, occasional weekend seminars and summer colloquiums and, if desired, attendance at courses in regular colleges."[81] Supported during the planning stages by the Ford Foundation and Carnegie Corporation, Empire State College hopes to reach two types of students: the alienated and the adult.

During the 1960s, the era of student unrest, considerable pressure developed from many students of the eighteen- to twenty-year-old age group who indicated they were turned off by the restrictive policies of the traditional campus-bound universities. Life and learning were inhibited by residential colleges, these students contended, and alternatives for one's education and development which permitted and encouraged self-direction were called for. Empire State College offers one such alternative.

In addition, the college looks toward a second broad group of students. This group includes housewives, workers, businessmen, and others who have either dropped out of college or never had the time or opportunity to attend institutions of higher learning. Chancellor Boyer expressed belief that the initial push for admission would come from this group.

Educators have been carefully watching development of the Empire State College and already a number of other states have undertaken feasibility and planning studies. During the summer and fall of 1971 the University of Maine began working on a plan to offer higher education on a statewide basis. Directed initially toward lower division students, the University of Maine plan calls for the use of "television, radio, even tape cassettes, with individual instruction every three weeks."[82] Circuit-riding professors would periodically visit the nine university campuses and provide face-to-face instruction. Of the external degree program, the University of Maine chancellor commented: ". . . education will have to decide whether to reach people where they are or go the elitist approach. . . . I don't think society is going to stand for more of the same—more buildings, more campus."[83]

The state of New Jersey, after a long period of deferred development of higher education has recently also moved into a period of expansion and has announced plans for a nonresidential college. While the new institution, Thomas A. Edison College, is still in early stages of development, there seems little doubt it will resemble the New York regents' external degree program, relying heavily upon proficiency examinations. In an unusual consortium arrangement, the Antioch-based "university without walls" program will coordinate activity of some twenty institutions in an attempt to diversify and enrich undergraduate education.

It must be remembered that not all special programs for adults focus on a degree. Supported by a Title 1 H.E.A. grant, Mohawk Valley Community College (Utica, New York) coordinated a consortium project in 1977 entitled a "Model Community Development Curriculum and Training Center." The year-long project enabled the college to conduct a series of leadership skill courses for members of upstate New York neighborhood organizations, labor unions, and public service agencies. As important as the curriculum itself, the coalition of colleges, community organizations, and public agencies continues to search out ways to bring new vitality to the urban communities of the central New York corridor. At this writing, the coalition is planning a major Vista Volunteer program unique in its design. The project will not only place volunteers in manpower-short community organizations, but will additionally enable the volunteers to receive intensive training in community dynamics. If successful, the project may well affect the national course and content of domestic voluntary action programs sponsored by the federal government.

Finally, according to many, the overriding consideration for lifelong learning at the collegiate level must be vocational training and economic development. Powerful economic and social forces support this view. Problems of unemployment, resource scarcity, inflation, the environment, and energy all suggest colleges and universities are inescapably linked to a resolution of these material questions if America is to enjoy the freedom in the twenty-first century that it takes for granted today. Yet, that freedom is not simply a matter of historical abundance. It is the product of a unique socialization—a process which values citizenship. The principles of citizenship are found in a liberal arts curriculum rather than in vocational training. It is the prospect of coexistence, the legitimacy of both liberal and vocational learning which may yet see the American people through the ominous decades ahead.

Conclusions

Looking back at the development of higher adult education during the last half-century, from the time the University of Wisconsin helped reform the university's relationship with the public to the present, what trends emerge? Knowles has identified eight which have shaped the modern period:[84]

(1) *Enrollments increased, both absolutely and relatively.* In some institutions, particularly the urban universities, the adult evening enrollment increased so rapidly that the number of students in extension programs outnumbered the regular day population.

(2) *The scope of university adult education services has greatly broadened.* In addition to such traditional extension services as extension classes, correspondence work,

lectures, and traveling libraries, from the 1920s on, radio, television, short courses, community development, and a variety of other services have emerged.

(3) *There was movement in the direction of a broader and special adult curriculum, which took into account adult experiences.* Traditionally, the curriculum of higher education and the short-lived English extension movement in America was built around an academic, rather than a problem-solving, organization of knowledge. Starting with the Wisconsin Idea and intensifying during and after World War II, efforts were made, first to organize adult learning into a "sequence in which past education is integrated with a plan of organized instruction . . . to produce a unified, cumulative but individualized outcome. . . ,"[85] and secondly to "find some symbol (certificates, A. A. degrees) that would give recognition to the achievement of this outcome."[86]

(4) *Increasingly, administrative responsibility for higher adult education has become centralized.* Whereas before the turn of the century much of what has been described as higher adult education was undertaken on the initiative of individual faculty members and academic departments, but increasingly during the past half-century extension departments, divisions, evening colleges, and summer sessions have coordinated adult educational programs. James Carey has suggested the divisions have evolved in a "growth cycle" pattern ranging from the initial departmental domination stage to a mature stage of assimilation within the university administrative structure.[87]

(5) *Financial support of higher adult education, both in absolute amounts and relative to the total budget, has increased.* Although higher adult education has for a half-century or more been expected to pay its own way, nevertheless "extension has been gradually gaining an increasing share of the total university budget."[88] Whereas in 1930,

29 percent of the university extension organizations studied by John Morton accounted for more than 5 percent of their respective universities budgets, by 1951–52 some 40 percent of the extension units studied had passed the 5 percent budget figure.[89]

(6) *There has been a tendency for extension staffs to grow in size, stature, and differentiation of role.* Morton and Carey both found that the part-time staff administrator had given way to a hierarchy of personnel, often including a dean and seven to ten assistants with varying responsibilities. Many had "rank and tenure in the extension organization itself and about one-third [of these] in instructional departments."[90]

(7) *Physical facilities for university extension expanded and became increasingly differentiated.* In addition to administrative office space for an increasingly large staff, off-campus centers and residential conference centers, both on and off campus, were designed specifically for the adult education program. In addition, facilities were used cooperatively with other agencies such as the public schools, industrial plants, and libraries.

(8) *There emerged a methodology designed for the unique characteristics of the adult-learner.* From World War I forward, spurred on by research studies, "university extension personnel became increasingly experimental in their teaching practices."[91] The adult-learner was more frequently used in the planning of programs, and group discussion replaced the lecture-recitation method. This development was stimulated by professional organizations such as the National University Extension Association, the Association of University Evening Colleges, the Adult Education Association as well as such agencies as the Carnegie Corporation, the Kellogg Foundation, and the Center for the Study of Liberal Education for Adults, all of which were interested in special adult learning characteristics.

A number of other trends have appeared since the University of Wisconsin led American higher education toward a modern relationship with the public.

(1) *There has been a continuing use of higher adult education by the university for public relations purposes.* This was recognized at the earliest meetings of the NUEA and has since been reported by countless writers. James Crimi in his study of adult education activity of the liberal arts colleges reported that in every college and in almost every interview "the public relations value of an adult education program was described as a major advantage of the college. . . . 'Tremendous, tremendous!' was the comment of the president of one eastern college. . . ."[92]

(2) *The use of the evening college and the summer session for remedial work persists.* In many universities a substantial number of evening and summer session credit hours are earned by regular day students, many of whom are required to make up academic deficiencies.

(3) *With less fanfare than the state and private universities, the liberal arts colleges have also attempted to offer their resources to their communities.* Crimi reported in 1957 that 57.7 percent of the 404 private liberal arts colleges studied were engaged in some kind of adult education program.[93] The total number of adults served, however, about forty-five thousand, suggests the limited extent of their efforts. While these numbers have doubtless increased by the 1970s, the movement toward "career education" has created special problems for the liberal arts colleges which affect both the day and evening divisions.

What, then, is the nature of higher adult education in America? In a general sense there has been and continues to be a higher adult education movement, that is, a history of organized activity by people working toward a common goal. This movement has shown great variance in intensity. During the 1880s and early 1890s higher adult education was promoted and conducted with an evangelical fervor. The enthusiasm and passion for service, though increasingly secular, characterized the early Wisconsin period as well. As the years passed, however, and extension became more firmly established and institutionalized, the use of it for public relations purposes gradually infringed upon the ideal. In response to crises, particularly the depression and World War II, one senses a return to the public service ideal. The ideal emerges in the present day as well. In the face of such problems as drug addiction, the universities have again extended their resources in an attempt to play a role in community life. Since the Wisconsin period, however, these efforts have been sporadic and essentially reactive rather than preventative. This cyclical nature, vitality and lethargy, may well not be a unique characteristic to those who study phenomena of social and institutional movements, though it would appear to be fundamental to adult higher education.

In addition, adult education at the college and university has been and continues to be, for the most part, a peripheral activity. Service is not just one of the three major functions of the university, joining teaching and research. It is clearly and accurately described as the third function and expected to be self-supporting. As a third and often marginal activity, it suffers from confusion of purpose. While on one hand it is motivated by the loftiest of ideals, yet, upon sober reflection, it acknowledges, often without regret, the public relations and budgetary objectives which permeate its activities.

Finally, is projection of the future development of higher adult education possible? The answer to that question lies in the purpose of higher education itself.

The purpose of the college and university of the past was rather clearly defined. As far back as the era of the High Middle Ages, the universities had what we now call "clearly defined goals." The university at Salerno in Italy sought to train individuals in the art of medicine, while the University of Bologna specialized in the teaching of Roman law, and the University of Paris was a center for theological instruction.

Early institutions of higher learning in the New World colonies, like their model institutions in England (Oxford and Cambridge), existed for the purpose of liberally educating prospective Protestant clergymen. As the colonies approached independence, new purposes became evident, such as the preparation of gentlemen for legal and political leadership. As the nation grew in population and size, strong social, economic, and technological pressures forced higher education to reform along more utilitarian lines. Since the rise of the university in America during the last quarter of the nineteenth century, great confusion has existed as to its role in society. This confusion, reported by Flexner,[94] Hutchins,[95] and others, continues to the present day.

With this confusion further complicated by rapidly changing cultural patterns, it would seem impossible today to project in a specific way the role to be played by adult education during this period of intense introspection in American higher education. Clearly the coming decades will see higher education more and more dominated by public institutions in urban environments. The rapid growth of community colleges would seem to insure this. To the extent this is true, judging from the leadership given to higher adult education by public and urban universities from the Wisconsin period forward, on the one hand, and the modern community colleges on the other, there is reason to believe adult education will be an increasingly important feature in American post-secondary education.

A variety of scenarios could and, indeed, have been formulated,[96] suggesting ways in which higher education can best serve its community. These scenarios are based typically on population projections, changes in technology, social adjustments, such as increasing leisure time, as well as on social problems and economic necessity.

A. A. Liveright has described the College of Continuing Education of the mythological metropolis university as the "central spot for initiating the problem-solving processes in the city,"[97] with the potential student body and faculty being drawn from all segments of the community. Thomas Green has outlined a plan of post-secondary education which integrates a community's universities, two-year colleges, museums, art centers, adult education centers, as well as business and industrial training programs.[98]

Without discounting the importance or possibility of such developments in continuing education, there is also evidence that the philosophy and mode of operation of continuing education is affecting traditional patterns of undergraduate higher education itself. The hallowed tradition of four years of campus instruction immediately following twelve years of public school instruction is under attack. It is now being suggested that a year or two between high school and college may well enable the learner to achieve the maturity and direction needed to more fully benefit from his formal higher education.

Moreover, the idea that experience itself may well be educative is achieving respectability on college campuses. Field experience programs are more numerous than ever before and, in some cases, the university calendar has been adapted specifically for that purpose.

The trend away from supervision of students *in loco parentis* reflects further the acceptance of the eighteen- to twenty-two-year-old student as adult as his noncollegiate counterpart. All this suggests that the ideal of continuing education, learning as a life-long process without artificial chronological barriers, has begun to influence the pattern of American higher education. The external degree program described earlier perhaps best illustrates that development.

Ultimately, however, study of the progression of American higher education focuses less on the question of the need for continuing education than on the capacity and willingness of the public to support it. Of the capacity, perhaps one can be reasonably optimistic. Of the willingness, the thoughtful ordering of priorities has not yet become our greatest virtue.

Notes

Chapter 1

1. Merle Curti, *A History of American Civilization* (New York: Harper and Row, 1953), p. 364.

2. Max Lerner, *America as a Civilization* (New York: Simon and Shuster, 1957), p. 85.

3. Arthur M. Schlesinger, *Political and Social Growth of the United States—1852-1933* (New York: Macmillan Co., 1936), p. 131.

4. Ibid., p. 247.

5. Samuel Eliot Morison and Henry Steele Commager, *The Growth of the American Republic* (New York: Oxford University Press, 1942), pp. 511-12.

6. Curti, *History of American Civilization*, p. 235.

7. Ibid.

8. Morison and Commager, *Growth of the American Republic*, p. 512.

9. Harry Gehman Good, *A History of American Education* (New York: Macmillan Co., 1956), p. 233.

10. Donald G. Tewksbury, *The Founding of American Colleges and Universities Before the Civil War* (New York: Teachers' College, Columbia University Press, 1932), p. 55.

11. Robert E. Potter, *The Stream of American Education* (New York: American Book Co., 1967), p. 258.

12. Francis Wayland, quoted in Allen Nevins, *State Universities and Democracy* (Urbana: University of Illinois Press, 1962), p. 11.

13. Horace Greeley, quoted in Nevins, *State Universities and Democracy,* p. 11.

14. Frederick Rudolph, *The American College and University* (New York: Random House, 1962), p. 233.

15. Richard J. Storr, *Beginnings of Graduate Education in America* (Chicago: University of Illinois Press, 1953), p. 64.

16. Rudolph, *American College and University,* p. 252.

17. Good, *History of American Education,* p. 295.

18. Ibid., pp. 296–97.

19. Ibid., p. 300.

20. *Report of the Commissioner of Education, 1898–99,* vol. 2 (Washington, D.C.: Government Printing Office, 1900), pp. 1737–47.

21. John S. Brubacher and Willis Rudy, *Higher Education in Transition* (New York: Harper and Row, 1968), p. 63.

22. Ibid., pp. 63–64.

23. *Report of the Commissioner of Education, 1898–99,* vol. 2, p. 1662.

24. For a detailed study of the early years of the Johns Hopkins University and its leadership, see Hugh Hawkins, *Pioneer: A History of the Johns Hopkins University* (Ithaca: Cornell University Press, 1960), chaps. 1-10.

25. Charles W. Eliot, quoted in Brubacher and Rudy, *Higher Education in Transition,* p. 183.

Chapter 2

1. C. Hartley Grattan, *In Quest of Knowledge* (New York: Association Press, 1955), p. 135.

2. Charles A. Beard and Mary A. Beard, *A Basic History of the United States* (New York: Doubleday, Doran, and Co., 1944), p. 67.

3. Morison and Commager, *Growth of the American Republic,* p. 114.

4. Curti, *History of American Civilization,* p. 159.

5. "The Publisher's Desk," *Munsey's Magazine* 13, no. 1 (April 1895): 103.

6. Curti, *History of American Civilization,* p. 414.

7. Grattan, *In Quest of Knowledge,* p. 144.

8. Good, *History of American Education*, p. 425.

9. Morison and Commager, *Growth of the American Republic*, p. 312.

10. Curti, *History of American Civilization*, p. 412.

11. Carl Bode, *The American Lyceum: Town Meeting of the Mind* (New York: Oxford University Press, 1956), p. 13.

12. For a text of Holbrook's organizational plan as well as his rationale, see C. Harley Gratton, ed., *American Ideas About Adul: Education* (New York: Columbia University Press, 1959), chap. 4.

13. John S. Noffsinger, *Correspondence Schools, Lyceums, and Chautauquas* (New York: Macmillan Co., 1926), pp. 101–2.

14. Ibid., p. 102.

15. For an account of the national lyceum and its proposals toward public education, see Cecil B. Hayes, *The American Lyceum, Its History and Contribution to Education*, U.S. Dept. of Interior Bulletin, no. 12 (Washington, D.C.: Government Printing Office, 1932).

16. Noffsinger, *Correspondence Schools, Lyceums, and Chautauquas*, p. 105.

17. Bode, *American Lyceum*, p. 249.

18. Grattan, *In Quest of Knowledge*, pp. 83–84.

19. Bode, in *American Lyceum*, elaborates on the relationship between the lyceum and the mechanics' institute.

20. Grattan, *In Quest of Knowledge*, p. 150.

21. Ibid., p. 201.

22. *Report of the Commissioner of Education, 1885–86* (Washington, D.C.: Government Printing Office, 1887), p. 480.

23. Williard S. Elsbree, *The American Teacher* (New York: American Book Co., 1939), p. 155.

24. Potter, *Stream of American Education*, p. 257.

25. Malcolm S. Knowles, *The Adult Education Movement in the United States* (New York: Holt, Rinehart and Winston, 1962), p. 15.

26. Edward Weeks, *The Lowells and Their Institute* (Boston: Atlantic Monthly Press, 1966), p. 10.

27. Ibid., p. 11.

28. Ibid., pp. 36–37.

29. Ibid., p. 44.

30. "The Lowell Offering," *Atlantic Monthly* 67, no. 402 (April 1891): 570–71.

31. Peter Cooper's letter to the trustees accompanying the deed, quoted in J. M. Buckley, "The Cooper Institute," *Chautauquan* 6, no. 7 (April 1884): 398.

32. Peter Cooper, quoted in Lloyd Bryce, "The Example of a Great Life," *North American Review* 150, no. 413 (April 1891): 419.

33. Peter Cooper, quoted in Buckley, "Cooper Institute," p. 398.

34. Ibid., p. 399.

35. Buckley, "Cooper Institute," p. 399.

36. Nathaniel Peffer, *New Schools for Older Adults* (New York: Macmillan Co., 1926), pp. 30–43.

37. Noffsinger, *Correspondence Schools, Lyceums, Chautauquas*, p. 4.

38. Ossian MacKenzie, E. L. Christensen, and Paul Rigby, *Correspondence Instruction in the United States* (New York: McGraw-Hill Book Co., 1968), pp. 24–25.

39. Ossian MacKenzie and E. L. Christensen, *The Changing World of Correspondence Study* (University Park: Pennsylvania State University Press, 1971), p. 29.

40. Ibid., p. 28.

41. MacKenzie et al., *Correspondence Instruction in the United States*, p. 25.

42. "The Correspondence University." *Harper's Weekly* 27 (27 October 1883): 676.

43. Dean Graham, *Bulletin of the Graduate and Non-Resident Department* (Illinois Wesleyan University, 1904), quoted in Walter S. Bittner and Hervey F. Mallory, *University Teaching by Mail* (New York: Macmillan Co., 1933), p. 15.

44. Bittner and Mallory, *University Teaching by Mail*, p. 16.

45. *Report of the Commissioner of Education, 1898–99*, vol. 2, pp. 1564–65.

46. Ibid. pp. 1564–1565.

47. Ibid. pp. 1564–1565.

48. Excerpts of institutional catalogs, quoted in *Report of the Commissioner of Education, 1898–99*, vol. 2, pp. 1566–81.

49. Ibid., p. 1631.

50. Noffsinger, *Correspondence Schools, Lyceums, and Chautauquas*, pp. 11–12.

51. Ibid., p. 13.

Chapter 3

1. William Rainey Harper, "The Founder of the Chautauqua Movement," *Outlook* 54, no. 13 (26 September 1896): 546.

2. Ibid., p. 548.

3. Jesse L. Hurlbut, *The Story of Chautauqua* (New York: G. P. Putnam's Sons, 1921), pp. 15–17.

4. Ibid., p. 18.

5. John H. Vincent, *The Chautauqua Movement* (Boston: Chautauqua Press, 1886), p. 19.

6. Ibid., p. 75.

7. Hurlbut, *Story of Chautauqua*, p. 119.

8. *Development of University Extension*, Regents' Bulletin no. 5 (Albany: University of the State of New York, 1893), p. 210.

9. Ibid., p. 123.

10. *Society to Encourage Studies at Home* (Cambridge: Riverside Press, 1897), p. 92.

11. Hurlbut, *Story of Chautauqua*, pp. 134–36.

12. Ibid., pp. 149–50.

13. *Chautauquan* 3, no. 3(December 1882): 161–77.

14. Edward Everett Hale, "The Chautauqua Literary and Scientific Circle," *Century* 9, no. 1 (November 1885): 147–50.

15. "C.L.S.C. Graduates—The Class of 1885," *Chautauquan* 6, no. 5 (February 1886): 52.

16. Theodore Flood, "Editor's Outlook," *Chautauquan* 9, no. 1 (October 1888): 52.

17. "Local Circles," *Chautauquan* 3, no. 3 (December 1882): 163.

18. Hale, "Chautauqua Literary and Scientific Circle," p. 149.

19. Herbert Baxter Adams, "Summer Schools and University Extension," *Education in the United States,* vol. 2, edited by Nicholas Murray Butler (Albany: J. B. Lyon, 1900), p. 827.

20. Ibid., p. 827.

21. R. S. Holmes, "The Chautauqua University," *Chautauquan* 5, no. 3 (December 1884): 170.

22. "The Twelfth Chautauqua Assembly," *Chautauquan* 6, no. 1 (October 1885): 43.

23. Ibid., p. 43.

24. Ibid., p. 43.

25. Adams, "Summer Schools and University Extension," in Butler, *Education in the United States,* p. 828.

26. "The Summer Assemblies," *Chautauquan* 5, no. 10 (July 1885): 604.

27. Marcel, "To the Editor of the Nation," *Nation* 49 (10 October 1889): 290.

28. Vincent, *Chautauqua Movement*, pp. 87–88.

29. Editor, *Nation* 49 (19 September 1889): 232.

30. C.A.W., "A Plea for Chautauqua," *Nation* 49 (31 October 1889): 350.

31. S. E. Raybould, "University Extra-Mural Education in Great Britain," from *Universities in Adult Education* (Paris: UNESCO, 1952), pp. 27–28.

32. Thomas Kelly, *A History of Adult Education in Great Britain* (Liverpool: Liverpool University Press, 1962), pp. 216–17.

33. Ibid., pp. 218–19.

34. Ibid., p. 220.

35. Ibid., p. 220.

36. James Stuart, "A Letter on University Extension" (Cambridge 1871), p. 7, quoted in Kelly, *History of Adult Education in Great Britain*, p. 221.

37. Kelly, *History of Adult Education in Great Britain*, p. 222.

38. Herbert Baxter Adams, "University Extension in Great Britain," from *Report of the Commissioner of Education, 1889–99*, vol. 1 (Washington, D.C.: Government Printing Office, 1900), p. 995.

39. Ibid., p. 997.

40. Ibid., p. 997.

41. Ibid., p. 998.

42. Ibid., p. 999.

43. Ibid., p. 1007.

44. Ibid., p. 1000.

45. Herbert Baxter Adams, "University Extension in England," *Report of the Commissioner of Education, 1885–86* (Washington, D.C.: Government Printing Office, 1887), p. 749.

46. Ibid., p. 749.

47. Kelly, *History of Adult Education in Great Britain*, p. 234.

48. Adams, "University Extension in England," p. 748.

49. J. M. Vincent, "Herbert B. Adams, a Biographical Sketch," and Richard T. Ely, "A Sketch of the Life and Services of Herbert Baxter Adams," from *Herbert Baxter Adams*, Johns Hop-

kins Studies in Historical and Political Science, vol. 23 (Baltimore: Johns Hopkins Press, 1902), pp. 9–49.

50. Herbert Baxter Adams, "University Extension and Its Leaders," from *Regents' Bulletin* extension no. 5, no. 21 (Albany: University of the State of New York, May 1895), pp. 206–14.

51. Ibid., pp. 215–16.

52. Ibid., pp. 216–17.

53. Ibid., p. 222.

54. Herbert Baxter Adams, "A Letter to the Springfield Republican," quoted in *Library Journal* 12, no. 11 (November 1887): 512.

55. J. N. Larned, "To the Buffalo Courier," *Library Journal*, 12, no. 11 (November 1887): 513.

56. J. N. Larned, "An Experiment in University Extension," *Library Journal*, 13, nos. 3–4 (March-April 1888): 75.

57. Ibid., pp. 75–76.

58. Adams, *University Extension and Its Leaders*, p. 218.

59. "State Leadership," *University Extension Bulletin*, no. 1 (Albany: University of the State of New York, November 1891), p. 7.

60. Ibid., p. 8.

61. Ibid., pp. 8-9.

62. "The University Extension Law," Laws of 1891, Chapter 303, quoted in *University Extension Bulletin*, no. 1 (November 1891):pp.10–11.

63. "Plan of Work," *University Extension Bulletin*, no. 2. (September 1892), pp. 55–67.

64. Adams, *University Extension and Its Leaders*, pp. 220–221.

65. Willis Boughton, "University Extension," *Arena* 4. no. 22 (September 1891): 457.

66. "Editorial," *School and College* 1, no. 2 (February 1892): 108–9.

67. Charles B. Stover, "The Neighborhood Guild in New York, *Johns Hopkins University Studies in Historical & Political Science,* vol. 7 (Baltimore: Johns Hopkins University, 1889), pp. 65–67.

68. Morrison I. Swift, *The Plan of a Social University* (Philadelphia: Social University Monographs, n.d.), p. 4.

69. Ibid., p. 29.

70. "Ten Years Report of the ASUET, 1890–1900" (Phil-

adelphia 1901) from C. Hartley Grattan (ed.), *American Ideas About Adult Education* (New York: Columbia University Press, 1959), p. 102–10.

71. "What Has the American Society Accomplished?" *University Extension*, 2, no. 6 (December 1892): 161.

72. Nathaniel Butler, "University Extension Class—Courses of the University of Chicago," *University Extension*, 4, no.6 (December 1894): 171.

73. Ibid., p. 172.

74. Ibid., p. 174.

75. Nathaniel Butler, "The University of Chicago and University Extension," *University Extension*, 3, no. 8 (February 1894): 246–47.

76. Ibid., p. 248.

77. T. W. Goodspeed, *A History of the University of Chicago.* (Chicago: University of Chicago Press, 1916), p. 247.

78. Ibid., p. 150.

79. Grattan, *In Quest of Knowledge*, pp. 189–190.

80. John Stecklein et al., *The Summer Session* (Minneapolis: University of Minnesota, 1958), p. 9.

81. Ibid., p. 10.

82. Ibid. p. 10.

83. Clarence A. Schoenfeld, *The American University in Summer* (Madison: University of Wisconsin Press, 1967), pp. 13–14.

84. "Summer Schools," *Extension Bulletin*, no. 25 (Albany: University of the State of New York, 1898), pp. 289, 306.

85. "Summer Schools, 1900," *Home Education Department Bulletin*, no. 36 (Albany: University of the State of New York, 1900), p. 3.

86. "Report of Summer Schools," *Home Education Department Bulletin*, no. 30 (Albany: University of the State of New York, July 1889), p. 3.

87. Adams, cited in Grattan, *In Quest of Knowledge*, p. 191.

88. Baldwin M. Woods and Helen V. Hammarberg, "University Extension in the United States of America," from *Universities in Adult Education*, p. 131.

89. Grattan, *In Quest of Knowledge*, p. 191.

Chapter 4

1. Curti, *History of American Civilization*, p. 516.

2. Ibid., p. 517.

3. Ibid., pp. 523–24.

4. Frederick C. Howe, *Wisconsin, An Experiment in Democracy* (New York: Charles Scribner's Sons, 1912), p. vii.

5. Merle Curti and Vernon Carstensen, *The University of Wisconsin, 1848–1925,* vol. 2 (Madison: University of Wisconsin, 1949), p. 4.

6. Ibid., p. 4.

7. Ibid., p. 5.

8. Robert M. La Follette, *La Follette's Autobiography* (Madison: University of Wisconsin Press, 1960), pp. 14–15.

9. William Hard, "A University in Public Life," *Outlook* 86 (July 1907): 667.

10. Larry Gara, *A Short History of Wisconsin* (Madison: State Historical Society of Wisconsin, 1962), p. 201.

11. Charles McCarthy, *The Wisconsin Idea* (New York: Macmillan, 1912), p. 215.

12. Gara, *Short History of Wisconsin,* p. 201.

13. Belle Case La Follette and Lola La Follette, *Robert M. La Follette,* vol. 2 (New York: Macmillan, 1953), p. 161.

14. Ibid., pp. 162–63.

15. Ibid.

16. Charles Van Hise, "The University Extension Function in the Modern University," *NUEA Proceedings,* vol. 1 (Madison 1915), p. 24.

17. Ibid. p. 24.

18. Curti and Carstensen, *University of Wisconsin,* pp. 552–53.

19. Ibid., p. 554.

20. Van Hise to Austin W. Stultz, New York, 17 April 1905, President's Papers, quoted in Curti and Carstensen, *University of Wisconsin,* p. 554.

21. Curti and Carstensen, *University of Wisconsin,* p. 555.

22. Ibid., p. 556.

23. Legler Van Hise Letters, Oct. 2, 8 1906, President's Papers from Curti and Carstensen, *University of Wisconsin,* p. 557.

24. "Report of the Committee on Credit for University Extension Work," October 1906, from Curti and Carstensen, *University of Wisconsin,* p. 557.

25. Curti and Carstensen, *University of Wisconsin,* p. 558.

26. Reber to Van Hise, August 14, 1907, President's Papers, quoted in Curti and Carstensen, *University of Wisconsin,* p. 561.

27. Frederick M. Rosenstreter, *The Boundaries of the Cam-*

pus, A History of the Wisconsin Extension Division 1885–1945 (Madison: University of Wisconsin Press, 1957), p. 52.

28. Ibid., p. 53.

29. Ibid., p. 65.

30. Ibid., p. 67.

31. Van Hise, "University Extension Function," p. 15.

32. Ford McGregor, "The Municipal Reference Bureau," *NUEA Proceedings,* vol. 1, March 1915, p. 132.

33. Ibid., p. 137.

34. Van Hise, "University Extension Function," p. 19.

35. Ibid., p. 19.

36. Ibid., pp. 19–20.

37. Mary Burchard Orvis, "Wisconsin's Package Libraries," *Independent,* 72, no. 3325, August 22, 1912, p. 436.

38. Ibid.

39. Almere Scott, "Replies to Specific Inquiries and the Circulation of Traveling Package Libraries," *NUEA Proceedings,* 1, March 1915, p. 146.

40. Ibid., p. 147.

41. Andrew H. Melville, "The Field Work in Extension," *NUEA Proceedings,* March 1915, p. 63.

42. Ibid., p. 64.

43. Ibid., p. 64.

44. Louis E. Reber, "Self-supporting and Contributory Fees in the University Extension Budget," *NUEA Proceedings,* April 1917, pp. 12–13.

45. Ibid., p. 13.

46. Abstracted from Louis E. Reber, "The Scope of University Extension and Its Organization and Subdivisions," *NUEA Proceedings,* March 1915, p. 33.

47. Lincoln Steffens, "Sending a State to College," *American Magazine* 67 (February 1909): 361.

48. Grattan, *In Quest of Knowledge,* p. 191.

49. Figures cited by Van Hise, "University Extension Function," pp. 22–23.

50. Smith-Lever Act of 1914, quoted in Van Hise, "University Extension Function," pp. 23–24.

51. "Extending University Extension," *Independent* 74, no. 3363 (May 15, 1913): 1104.

52. Richard R. Price, "Minnesota's University Weeks," *NUEA Proceedings,* March 1915, pp. 160–61.

53. Ibid., p. 159.

54. Ibid., p. 163.

55. Ibid., pp. 163–64.

56. Ibid., p. 159.

57. Gerhard A. Gesell, "Discussion," *NUEA Proceedings,* March 1915, pp. 154–55.

58. "Extending University Extension," p. 1104.

59. Ira Howerth, "Extension in the West," *NUEA Proceedings,* April 1917, p. 76.

60. Ibid., p. 76.

61. Ibid., pp. 76–77.

62. Ibid., p. 76.

63. F. F. Nalder, "The Opportunity and Demand for University Extension," *School and Society* 6, no. 143 (Sept. 22, 1917): 345.

64. Ibid., p. 345.

65. Ibid., pp. 345–46.

66. Ibid., pp. 347–49.

67. Brubacher and Rudy, *Higher Education in Transition,* pp. 106–7.

68. William Henderson, "General Education through Extension," *NUEA Proceedings,* March 1915, p. 42.

69. Ibid., p. 45.

70. Ibid., pp. 40–41.

71. Louis Wilson, "Extension Work in the Southeast," *NUEA Proceedings,* April 1917, pp. 77–78.

72. Ibid., p. 77.

73. Ibid., pp. 78–79.

74. Ibid., pp. 79–80.

75. C. B. Robertson, "Types of University Extension Development and Present-day Tendencies in the Eastern States," *NUEA Proceedings,* April 1917, p. 72.

76. Ibid.

77. Ibid., p. 73.

78. Ibid., p. 78.

79. John Angus Burrell, *A History of Adult Education at Columbia University* (New York: Columbia University Press, 1954), p. 3.

80. Egbert, quoted in Burrell, *History of Adult Education,* p. 19.

81. Ibid., pp. 24–52. See also James Egbert, "Class Lecture Instruction," *NUEA Proceedings,* March 1915, pp. 83–90.

82. Reber, "Scope of University Extension," p. 26.

83. Ibid.

84. Ibid.

85. A. J. Klein, "Report of the Treasurer," *NUEA Proceedings,* April 1920, p. 106.

Chapter 5

1. Knowles, *Adult Education Movement,* p. 76.

2. Ibid., p. 77.

3. Ibid., p. 77–78.

4. Grattan, *In Quest of Knowledge,* p. 195.

5. W. S. Bittner, quoted in James Creese, *The Extension of University Teaching* (New York American Association for Adult Education, 1941), p. 58.

6. Creese, *Extension of University Teaching,* p. 57.

7. Ibid., pp. 57–58.

8. George F. Zook, R. A. Kent, and A. Caswell Ellis, "Evening and Other Part-time Education," *North Central Association Quarterly,* 4 no. 2, (September 1929): 238.

9. These institutions were, in addition to the previously mentioned schools, the College of the City of New York, Hunter College, the University of Cincinnati, the University of the City of Toledo, the Municipal University of Akron, the College of the City of Detroit, and the Municipal University of Wichita. All but the University of Louisville maintained an evening session.

10. Parke R. Kolbe, *Urban Influences on Higher Education in England and the United States* (New York: Macmillan, 1928), pp. 137–39.

11. Ibid., p. 151.

12. Ibid., p. 150.

13. John R. Morton, *University Extension* (Birmingham: University of Alabama Press, 1953), p. 15.

14. Ibid., p. 15.

15. "Historical Introduction," *Association of Urban Universities Proceedings,* 1945, p. 5.

16. John P. Dyer, *Ivory Towers in the Market Place* (Indianapolis: Bobbs–Merrill Co., 1956), p. 38.

17. Ibid., pp. 38–39.

18. Ibid., p. 190.

19. Ibid., p. 188.

20. Ibid., p. 189.

21. John H. Beatty, "The Interest of Employers in Study Pro-

grams of Their Employees," *Association of Urban Universities Proceedings*, November 1927, pp. 36–41.

22. Kolbe, *Urban Influences on Higher Education*, p. 189.

23. "Significant Features of Adult Classes," *Association of Urban Universities Proceedings*, November 1928, p. 165.

24. George F. Zook, "Standards of Evening Sessions in Colleges and Universities of the North Central Association," *Association of Urban Universities Proceedings*, November 1928, p. 38.

25. Kolbe, *Urban Influences on Higher Education*, p. 191.

26. W. W. Folwell, quoted in Walter Crosby Eells, *The Junior College* (Boston: Houghton Mifflin Co., 1931), p. 45.

27. Ibid.

28. Ibid.

29. William Rainey Harper, "President's Annual Report," *Decennial Publications of the University of Chicago* 1 (Chicago: University of Chicago, 1903): xcvi.

30. Eells, *Junior College*, p. 52.

31. J. R. Angell, "The Junior College Movement in High Schools," *School Review* 23 (May 1915): 289–302.

32. Eells, *Junior College*, p. 53.

33. Walter Crosby Eells, *American Junior Colleges* (Washington, D.C.: American Council on Education, 1940), p. 13.

34. W. C. Wood, quoted in Eells, *Junior College*, p. 107.

35. Ibid., pp. 75–80.

36. F. W. Thomas, "A Study of Functions of the Public Junior College and the Extent of Their Realization in California," summarized in Eells, *Junior College*, p. 191.

37. Ibid.

38. McKenzie, quoted in Eells, *Junior College*, p. 236.

39. L. R. Alderman, "College and University Extension Helps in Adult Education," *Bureau of Education Bulletin*, no. 3 (Washington, D.C.: Government Printing Office, 1928), pp. 4–12.

40. Eells, *Junior College*, p. 243.

41. Roy W. Goddard, "Junior College Serves Community Needs," *Junior College Journal*, no. 6 (March 1934): 308–11; Walter C. Eells, "Adult Education in California Junior Colleges," *Junior College Journal* 5, no. 8 (May 1935): 437–48.

42. David R. Metzler, "Student Opinion on Adult Education," *Junior College Journal*, no. 7 (April 1933): 347 50; Ruth Fowler and David Bucharest, "The Junior Evening College Student," *Junior College Journal* vj, no. 6 (February 1940): 318–20.

43. C. L. Robbins, "Small Junior Colleges and Adult Educa-

tion," *Junior College Journal* 1, no. 9 (June 1931): 555–59; George F. Zook, "Junior Colleges and Adult Education" 4, no. 6 (March 1934): 279–80.

44. Carroll Atkinson, *Radio Extension Courses Broadcast for Credit* (Boston: Meador Publishing Co., 1941), p. 12.

45. W. H. Lighty, "Educational Radio Broadcasting as a Form of Extra-Mural Teaching," *NUEA Proceedings,* April 1923, p. 112.

46. Ibid., p. 112.

47. Ibid., p. 112.

48. Ibid., p. 113.

49. Ibid., pp. 113–14.

50. Ibid., pp. 116–17.

51. W. H. Lighty, "Report on Radio Broadcasting," *NUEA Proceedings,* May 1924, p. 20.

52. N. C. Miller, "Symposium on Teaching Radio Theory by Correspondence Instruction," *NUEA Proceedings,* April-May 1925, p. 128.

53. J. F. Wostrel, "Teaching Radio Theory—Class Instruction," *NUEA Proceedings,* April-May 1925, p. 131.

54. Ibid., p. 133.

55. J. W. Scroggs, "Seventh Session," *NUEA Proceedings,* April-May 1925, p. 128.

56. W. H. Lighty, "Report of the Committee on Radio Broadcasting," *NUEA Proceedings,* June 1926, p. 78.

57. B. C. Riley, "Some Problems of University State Stations," *NUEA Proceedings,* May 1929, p. 118.

58. Ibid., pp. 118–19.

59. Alderman, "College and University Extension Helps," pp. 4–12.

60. W. T. Middlebrook, "Educational Sponsorship of Radio Programs," *Education on the Air* (Columbus: Ohio State University, 1930), p. 38.

61. Atkinson, *Radio and Extension Courses Broadcast for Credit,* pp. 41–45.

62. E. M. Foster et al., *Statistics of Higher Education,* Bulletin 1935, no. 2 (Washington, D.C.: Government Printing Office, 1937), pp. 1–27.

63. F. W. Shockley, "Report of the Committee on Statistics and Research," *NUEA Proceedings,* May 1935, p. 74.

64. Curti, *History of American Civilization,* pp. 673–74.

65. Morison and Commager, *Growth of the American Republic,* p. 613.

66. "Salient Features of Current Programs for Adults in Member Institutions," *Association of Urban Universities Proceedings,* 1933, p. 105.

67. Ibid., p. 105.

68. Lewis Wilson, "The Emergency College Program in New York State," *Association of Urban Universities Proceedings,* 1933, p. 61.

69. Ibid., p. 62.

70. Philip Nash, "Cooperation with Other Institutions," *Association of Urban Universities Proceedings,* 1934, p. 81.

71. C. S. Marsh, "The Educational Program in the Civilian Conservation Corps," *Association of Urban Universities Proceedings,* 1934, p. 36.

72. Ibid., p. 36.

73. Ibid., p. 37.

74. C. S. Marsh, "The CCC Educational Program," *NUEA Proceedings,* May 1935, p. 62.

75. Ibid., p. 62.

76. Ibid., pp. 63–64.

77. Howard W. Oxley, "University Extension in CCC Camp Education," *NUEA Proceedings,* May 1936, p. 43.

78. Ibid., pp. 45–46.

79. Ibid., p. 46.

80. Ibid., p. 46.

81. Ibid., p. 47.

82. Ibid., p. 47.

83. Committee report, quoted in Elmer Scott, "The Program of the American Association of Adult Education," *NUEA Proceedings,* May 1929, p. 40.

84. Dyer, *Ivory Towers,* p. 39.

85. Russell Grumman, *University Extension in Action* (Chapel Hill: University of North Carolina Press, 1946), p. 143.

86. Stanley J. Drazek et al., *Extending Horizons ... Continuing Education* (Washington, D.C.: North Washington Press, 1965), p. 26.

87. Ibid., p. 25.

88. Grumman, *University Extension,* p. 146.

89. Frederick J. Kelly, "What Can the Evening School Do Now as to Assist in the Preparation for Defense and Reconstruc-

tion?" *Association of Urban Universities Proceedings,* 1941, p. 67.

90.   Drazek et al., *Expanding Horizons,* p. 27.

Chapter 6

1.   Theodore J. Shannon and Clarence A. Schoenfeld, *University Extension* (New York: Center of Applied Research in Education, 1965), p. 25.

2.   Clayton D. Hutchins and Albert R. Munse, *Federal Funds for Education, 1950–51 and 1951–2* (Washington, D.C.: Government Printing Office, 1952), p. 69.

3.   Ibid., p. 69.

4.   Ibid., p. 69.

5.   Ibid., p. 69.

6.   Ibid., p. 69.

7.   "Education of Korean Veterans," *Higher Education,* 12, no. 5 (January 1956): 82.

8.   President Harry Truman, quoted in Hutchins and Munse, *Federal Funds,* p. 73.

9.   Bradford Morse, "The Veteran and His Education," *Higher Education* 16, no. 7 (March 1960): 3.

10.   Ibid.

11.   Lloyd E. Blauch, "Higher Education and the Federal Government," *Higher Education* 13, no. 4 (December 1956): 56.

12.   W. T. Frazier, "Federal Surplus Property for Education," *Higher Education* 12, no. 5 (January 1956): 81.

13.   Blauch, "Higher Education and the Federal Government," p. 56.

14.   "Changes in the College Housing Program," *Higher Education* 13, no. 1 (September 1956): 13.

15.   Studies at Wisconsin, Ohio State, University of Michigan, UCLA, and the University of Southern California were reported by Morse, "Veteran and His Education," p. 18.

16.   "G.I.s at Harvard. They are the Best Students in the College's History," *Life,* July 1946, reported in Morse, "Veteran and His Education," p. 18.

17.   A. H. Monk, "Veterans' Administration," *NUEA Proceedings,* April 1952, p. 23.

18.   Donald A. Bartoni, "Education of Military Personnel," *NUEA Proceedings,* May 1953, p. 32.

19.   Ibid., p. 31.

20.   Ralph J. Klein, "The University of Maryland's Overseas

Program," *Higher Education* vol. 13, no. 8 (April 1957): 154.

21. Ibid., p. 155.

22. Ibid., p. 155.

23. Loren Reid, "Speech in the Maryland Overseas Program," *Quarterly Journal of Speech* 42, no. 4 (December 1956): 382.

24. Klein, "University of Maryland's Overseas Program," p. 379.

25. Reid, "Speech in the Maryland Overseas Program," p. 379.

26. The two early centers were identified as West Virginia University's Jackson's Mill (1922), and George Williams College, Lake George Campus (1884) by Harold J. Alford, *Continuing Education in Action* (New York: John Wiley and Sons, 1965), pp. 129–33.

27. Ibid., p. 21.

28. President Coffman, "Bulletin of the University of Minnesota, President's Report for the Years 1932–34," 37 (1934): 25, quoted in Harold J. Alford, "The Evolution of an Idea: From Danish Folk High School to Residential Center for Continuing Education," *Continuing Education Report from the University of Chicago*, no. 18, 1969, without pagination.

29. Harold Benjamin, "The Center for Continuation Study at the University of Minnesota," *NUEA Proceedings*, May 1937, p. 107.

30. Ibid., p. 107.

31. Ibid., p. 108.

32. Ibid., p. 108.

33. Alford, *Continuing Education*, p. 17.

34. Ibid., p. 18.

35. John A. Hannah, quoted in Alford, *Continuing Education*, p. 21.

36. Helen Hammarberg and Robert Schacht, "Conferences and Institutes," *NUEA Proceedings*, July 1951, p. 53.

37. Stanley C. Robinson, Carter Short, and J. D. Falls, "Conferences and Institutes," *NUEA Proceedings*, April 1952, p. 51.

38. Ibid., p. 52.

39. Ibid., p. 52.

40. Alford, *Continuing Education*, pp. 34–35.

41. Cyril O. Houle, "What is Continuing Education?" *Continuing Education Report*, no. 1 (1965), without pagination.

42. Ibid.

43. Donald A. Deppe, "The Director of Conference Programming: His Attitudes toward the Job Role," *Continuing Education Report,* no. 6 (1965), without pagination.

44. Ibid.

45. Laurence E. Devlin and Ann Litchfield, "Residential Program Data: A Statistical Description," *Continuing Education Report,* no. 15 (1967), without pagination.

46. Laurence E. Devlin and Ann Litchfield, "Residential Program Data: Implications for Practice," *Continuing Education Report,* no. 16 (1967), without pagination.

47. Cyril O. Houle, "University-level Continuing Education," *Continuing Education Report,* no. 7 (1965), without pagination.

48. Alford, *Continuing Education,* pp. 129–33.

49. Burton Paulu, "The Challenge of the 242 Channels," *NUEA Proccedings,* April 1952, p. 29.

50. Ibid., p. 30.

51. George N. Gordon, *Educational Television* (New York: Center for Applied Research in Education, 1965), p. 51.

52. Armand L. Hunter, "Recent Developments in Educational Television," *NUEA Proceedings* May 1953, p. 61.

53. Richard C. Hull, "First Educational TV Station Serves the Community," *Higher Education* 7, no. 15 (April 1951): 180.

54. Ibid., p. 180.

55. Gordon, *Educational Television,* pp. 52–53.

56. Ibid., p. 53.

57. Cyril Houle et al., *Television and the University,* Notes and Essays, no. 5 (Chicago: Center for the Study of Liberal Education for Adults, 1953), p. 206.

58. Otto G. Hoiberg and Roman Verhaslen, "Community Organization," *NUEA Proceedings,* April 1952, p. 48.

59. Ibid., p. 48.

60. Norris A. Hiett et al., "Report of the Division of Community Development," *NUEA Proceedings,* May 1956, p. 42.

61. Richard W. Poston, "Report of the Chairman, Division of Community Development," *NUEA Proceedings,* July 1958, p. 24.

62. Claud A. Bosworth, "Report of the Division of Community Development," *NUEA Proceedings,* April 1960, p. 40.

63. Poston, "Report of the Chairman," p. 24.

64. Howard Y. McClusky, "Community Development," in *Handbook of Adult Education in the United States,* edited by Mal-

colm S. Knowles (Chicago: Adult Education Association of the U.S.A., 1960), p. 424.

65. B. L. Coffindaffer, "West Virginia Appalachian Center," in *Proceedings of the Third NUEA Community Development Seminar,* June 1963, p. 108.

66. A. A. Liveright and Freda H. Goldman, *Significant Developments in Continuing Education,* Occasional Papers no. 12 (Boston: Center for the Study of Liberal Education for Adults, 1965), p. 18.

67. Ibid., p. 18.

68. Peter E. Siegle and James B. Whipple, *New Directions in Programming for University Adult Education* (Chicago: Center for the Study of Liberal Education for Adults, 1957), pp. 9–10.

69. Ibid., pp. 10–11.

70. Ibid., pp. 10–11.

71. Liveright and Goldman, *Significant Developments,* p. 19.

72. Ibid., p. 19.

73. Siegle and Whipple, *New Directions in Programming,* p. 85.

74. Brooklyn College, Syracuse University, the University of Oklahoma, Queens College, Goddard College, Johns Hopkins, and the San Francisco Theological Seminary.

75. A. A. Liveright and Roger De Crow, *New Directions in Degree Programs Especially for Adults* (Chicago: Center for the Study of Liberal Education for Adults, 1963), p. 26.

76. Ibid., p. 27.

77. Ibid., pp. 31–32.

78. John Walsh, "The Open University: Breakthrough for Britain?" *Science* 174 (12 November 1971): 675.

79. Ibid., p. 675.

80. Ibid., p. 675.

81. Ibid., p. 675.

82. "Maine to Try Taking College to Student," *New York Times,* 13 August 1971.

83. Ibid.

84. Knowles, *Adult Education Movement,* pp. 83–90.

85. Ibid., p. 85.

86. Ibid., p. 85.

87. James Carey, *Forms and Forces in University Adult Education* (Chicago: Center for the Study of Liberal Education for Adults, 1961).

88. Knowles, *Adult Education Movement,* p. 87.

89. John R. Morton, *University Extension in the United States* (Birmingham: University of Alabama Press, 1953), p. 97.

90. Knowles, *Adult Education Movement,* p. 86.

91. Ibid., p. 89.

92. James E. Crimi, *Adult Education in Liberal Arts Colleges* (Chicago: Center for the Study of Liberal Education for Adults, 1957), p. 30.

93. Ibid., pp. 1–38.

94. Abraham Flexner, *Universities: American, English, German* (New York: Oxford University Press, 1930).

95. Robert M. Hutchins, *The Higher Learning in America* (New Haven: Yale University Press, 1936).

96. Michael Marien, *Shaping the Future of American Education* (Syracuse: Education Policy Research Center, 1969) is just one of several useful, annotated bibliographies designed to acquaint the reader with the literature of educational futures.

97. A. A. Liveright, "Learning Never Ends: A Plan for Continuing Education," *Campus 1980,* edited by Alvin C. Eurich (New York: Dell Publishing Company, 1968), p. 151.

98. Thomas F. Green, *Post-Secondary Education in America: 1970–1990* (Syracuse: Syracuse University Press, 1969).

Bibliography

Books

Adams, Herbert Baxter, ed. *Johns Hopkins University Studies in Historical and Political Science*, Vol. 7. Baltimore: Johns Hopkins University Press, 1889.

Alford, Harold J. *Continuing Education in Action*. New York: John Wiley and Sons, 1968.

Atkinson, Carroll. *Radio Extension Courses Broadcast for Credit*. Boston: Meador Publishing Co., 1941.

Beard, Charles A., and Beard, Mary. *A Basic History of the United States*. New York: Doubleday, Doran, and Co., 1944.

Bittner, Walter S., and Mallory, Hervey F. *University Teaching by Mail*. New York: Macmillan, 1933.

Bode, Carl. *The American Lyceum: Town Meeting of the Mind*. New York: Oxford University Press, 1956.

Brubacher, John S. and Rudy, Willis. *Higher Education in Transition*. New York: Harper and Row, 1968.

Burrell, John Angus. *A History of Adult Education at Columbia University*. New York: Columbia University Press, 1954.

Butler, Nicholas Murray, ed. *Education in the United States*. 2 Vols. Albany: J. B. Lyon, 1900.

Carey, James. *Forms and Forces in University Adult Education*. Chicago: Center for the Study of Liberal Education for Adults, 1961.

195

Creese, James. *The Extension of University Teaching.* New York: American Association for Adult Education, 1941.

Curti, Merle. *A History of American Civilization.* New York: Harper and Row, 1953.

Curti, Merle, and Carstensen, Vernon. *The University of Wisconsin, 1848–1925.* Vol. 2. Madison: University of Wisconsin, 1949.

Drazek, Stanley J., et al. *Extending Horizons . . . Continuing Education.* Washington, D.C.: North Washington Press, 1965.

Dyer, John P. *Ivory Towers in the Market Place.* Indianapolis: Bobbs-Merrill Co., 1956.

Eells, Walter Crosby. *American Junior Colleges.* Washington, D.C.: American Council on Education, 1940.

Eells, Walter Crosby. *The Junior College.* Boston: Houghton Mifflin, 1931.

Elsbree, Williard S. *The American Teacher.* New York: American Book Co., 1939.

Eurich, Alvin C., ed. *Campus 1980.* New York: Dell Publishing Co., 1968.

Flexner, Abraham. *Universities: American, English, German.* New York: Oxford University Press, 1930.

Gara, Larry. *A Short History of Wisconsin.* Madison: State Historical Society of Wisconsin, 1962.

Good, Harry Gehman. *A History of American Education.* New York: Macmillan, 1956.

Goodspeed, T. W. *A History of the University of Chicago.* Chicago: University of Chicago Press, 1916.

Gordon, George E. *Educational Television.* New York: Center for Applied Research in Education, 1965.

Grattan, C. Hartley. *In Quest of Knowledge.* New York: Association Press, 1955.

Grattan, C. Hartley, ed. *American Ideas about Adult Education.* New York: Columbia University Press, 1959.

Grumman, Russell. *University Extension in Action.* Chapel Hill: University of North Carolina Press, 1946.

Hawkins, Hugh. *Pioneer: A History of the Johns Hopkins University.* Ithaca: Cornell University Press, 1960.

Howe, Frederick C. *Wisconsin: An Experiment in Democracy.* New York: Charles Scribner's Sons, 1912.

Hurlbut, Jesse L. *The Story of Chautauqua.* New York: G. P. Putnam's Sons, 1921.

Hutchins, Robert M. *The Higher Learning in America.* New Haven: Yale University Press, 1936.

Kelly, Thomas. *A History of Adult Education in Great Britain.* Liverpool: Liverpool University Press, 1962.

Knowles, Malcolm S. *The Adult Education Movement in the United States.* New York: Holt, Rinehart and Winston, 1962.

Knowles, Malcolm S., ed. *Handbook of Adult Education in the United States.* Chicago: Adult Education Association, 1960.

Kolbe, Parke R. *Urban Influences on Higher Education in England and the United States.* New York: Macmillan, 1928.

La Follette, Belle Case, and La Follette, Lola. *Robert M. La Follette.* Vol. 2. New York: Macmillan, 1953.

La Follette, Robert M. *La Follette's Autobiography.* Madison: University of Wisconsin Press, 1960.

Lerner, Max. *America as a Civilization.* New York: Simon and Shuster, 1957.

MacKenzie, Ossian, and Christensen, E. L. *The Changing World of Correspondence Study.* University Park: Pennsylvania State University Press, 1971.

MacKenzie, Ossian; Christensen, E. L., and Rigby, Paul. *Correspondence Instruction in the United States.* New York: McGraw-Hill, 1968.

McCarthy, Charles. *The Wisconsin Idea.* New York: Macmillan, 1912.

Morison, Samuel Eliot, and Commager, Henry Steele. *The Growth of the American Republic.* New York: Oxford University Press, 1942.

Morton, John R. *University Extension.* Birmingham: University of Alabama Press, 1953.

Nevins, Allen. *The State University and Democracy.* Urbana: University of Illinois Press, 1962.

Noffsinger, John S. *Correspondence Schools, Lyceums, and Chautauquas.* New York: Macmillan, 1926.

Peffer, Nathaniel. *New Schools for Older Adults.* New York: Macmillan, 1926.

Potter, Robert E. *The Stream of American Education.* New York: American Book Co., 1967.

Report of the Commissioner of Education, 1885–86. Washington, D.C.: Government Printing Office, 1887.

Report of the Commissioner of Education, 1898–99. Washington, D.C.: Government Printing Office, 1900.

Rosenstreter, Frederick M. *The Boundaries of the Campus: A History of the Wisconsin Extension Division, 1885–1945*. Madison: University of Wisconsin Press, 1957.

Rudolph, Frederick. *The American College and University*. New York: Random House, 1962.

Schlesinger, Arthur M. *Political and Social Growth of the United States—1852–1933*. New York: Macmillan, 1936.

Schoenfeld, Clarence A. *The American University in Summer*. Madison: University of Wisconsin Press, 1967.

Shannon, Theodore J. and Schoenfeld, Clarence A. *University Extension*. New York: Center for Applied Research in Education, 1965.

Society to Encourage Studies at Home. Cambridge: Riverside Press, 1897.

Stecklein, John, et al. *The Summer Session*. Minneapolis: University of Minnesota Press, 1958.

Storr, Richard J. *Beginnings of Graduate Education in America*. Chicago: University of Chicago Press, 1953.

Tewksbury, Donald G. *The Founding of American Colleges and Universities Before the Civil War*. New York: Columbia University Press, 1932.

Universities in Adult Education. Paris: UNESCO, 1952.

Vincent, John H. *The Chautauqua Movement*. Boston: Chautauqua Press, 1886.

Weeks, Edward. *The Lowells and Their Institute*. Boston: Atlantic Monthly Press, 1966.

Pamphlets, Proceedings, Reports

Adams, Herbert Baxter. "University Extension and Its Leaders." *Regents' Bulletin*, no. 21. Albany: University of the State of New York, 1895.

Adams, Herbert Baxter. "University Extension in England." *Report of the Commissioner of Education, 1885–86*. Washington, D.C.: Government Printing Office, 1887.

Adams, Herbert Baxter. "University Extension in Britain." *Report of the Commissioner of Education, 1898–99*, vol. 1. Washington, D.C.: Government Printing Office, 1900.

Alderman, L. R. "College and University Extension Helps in Adult Education." *Bureau of Education Bulletin*, no. 3. Washington, D.C. Government Printing Office, 1928.

Alford, Harold J. "The Evolution of an Idea: From Danish Folk

High School to Residential Center for Continuing Education."
Continuing Education Report from the University of Chicago,
no. 18, 1969.

Badger, Henry G.; Kelly, Frederick J.; and Blauch, Lloyd E. *Statistics in Higher Education, 1939–40 and 1941–42,* vol. 2.
Washington, D.C. Government Printing Office, 1944.

Bartoni, Donald A. "Education of Military Personnel." *NUEA Proceedings,* vol. 36, May 1953.

Beatty, John H. "The Interest of Employers in Study Programs of
Their Employees." *Association of Urban Universities Proceedings,* November 1927.

Benjamin, Harold. "The Center for Continuation Study at the University of Minnesota." *NUEA Proceedings,* vol. 20, May
1937.

Bosworth, Claud A. "Report of the Division of Community Development." *NUEA Proceedings,* vol. 43, 1960.

Coffindaffer, B. L. "West Virginia Appalachian Center." *Proceedings of the Third NUEA Community Development Seminar,*
1963.

Crimi, James E. *Adult Education in Liberal Arts College.* Chicago:
Center for the Study of Liberal Education for Adults, 1957.

Deppe, Donald A. "The Director of Conference Programming: His
Attitudes toward Job Role." *Continuing Education Report,* no.
6, 1965.

"Development of University Extension." *Regents' Bulletin,* no. 5.
Albany: University of the State of New York, 1893.

Devlin, Laurence E., and Litchfield, Ann. "Residential Program
Data: A Statistical Description." *Continuing Education Report,* no. 14, 1967.

Devlin, Laurence E., and Litchfield, Ann. "Residential Program
Data: Implications for Practice." *Continuing Education Report,* no. 16, 1967.

Foster, E. M. *Statistical Summary of Education, 1939–40.* Vol. 2.
Washington, D.C. Government Printing Office, 1943.

Foster, E. M., et al. *Statistics of Higher Education.* Bulletin 1935,
vol. 2. Washington, D.C.: Government Printing Office, 1937.

Gesell, Gerhard A. "Discussion." *NUEA Proceedings,* March 1915.

Green, Thomas F. *Post-Secondary Education in America 1970–
1990.* Syracuse: Syracuse University Press, 1969..

Hammarberg, Helen and Schacht, Robert. "Conferences and Institutes." *NUEA Proceedings,* vol. 34, July 1951.

Harper, William Rainey. "President's Annual Report." *Decennial Publications of the University of Chicago*, 1903, p. 179.

Hayes, Cecil B. *The American Lyceum, Its History and Contribution to Education.* U.S. Department of Interior bulletin no. 12. Washington, D.C.: Government Printing Office, 1932.

Henderson, William. "General Education Through Extension." *NUEA Proceedings*, March 1915, p. 42.

Hiett, Norris A., et al. "Report of the Division of Community Development." *NUEA Proceedings*, 1956.

"Historical Introduction." *Association of Urban Universities Proceedings*, 1945.

Hoiberg, Otto G. and Verhaslen, Rowan. "Community Organization." *NUEA Proceedings*, 1952.

Houle, Cyril O. "University-level Continuing Education." *Continuing Education Report*, no. 7, 1965.

Houle, Cyril O. "What Is Continuing Education?" *Continuing Education Report*, no. 1, 1965.

Houle, Cyril O., et al. *Television and the University.* Notes and Essays no. 5. Chicago: Center for the Study of Liberal Education for Adults, 1953.

Howerth, Ira. "Extension in the West." *NUEA Proceedings*, April 1917, p. 76.

Hunter, Armand L. "Recent Developments in Educational Television." *NUEA Proceedings*, vol. 36, 1953.

Hutchins, Clayton D., and Munse, Albert R. *Federal Funds for Education, 1950–51 and 1951–52.* Washington, D.C.: Government Printing Office, 1952.

Kelly, Frederick J. "What Can the Evening School Do Now to Assist in the Preparation for Defense and Reconstruction?" *Association of Urban Universities Proceedings*, 1941.

Klein, A. J. "Report of the Treasurer." *NUEA Proceedings.* April 1920.

Lighty, W. H. "Educational Radio Broadcasting as a Form of Extra-Mural Teaching." *NUEA Proceedings*, vol. 8, April 1923.

Lighty, W. H. "Report of the Committee on Radio Broadcasting." *NUEA Proceedings*, vol. 11, June 1926.

Lighty, W. H. "Report on Radio Broadcasting." *NUEA Proceedings*, vol. 9, May 1924.

Liveright, A. A. "Learning Never Ends: A Plan for Continuing

Education." *Campus 1980*, edited by Alvin C. Eurich. New York: Dell Publishing Co., 1968.

Liveright, A. A., and De Crow, Roger. *New Directions in Degree Programs Especially for Adults.* Chicago: Center for the Study of Liberal Education for Adults, 1963.

Liveright, A. A., and Goldman, Freda H. *Significant Developments in Continuing Education.* Occasional papers no. 12. Boston: Center for the Study of Liberal Education for Adults, 1965.

Marien, Michael. *Shaping the Future of American Education.* Syracuse: Educational Policy Research Center, 1969.

Marsh, C. S. "The CCC Educational Program." *NUEA Proceedings,* vol. 20, May 1935.

Marsh, C. S. "The Educational Program in the Civilian Conservation Corps." *Association of Urban Universities Proceedings,* 1934.

McClusky, Howard Y. "Community Development." *Handbook of Adult Education in the United States,* edited by Malcolm S. Knowles. Chicago: Adult Education Association, 1960.

McGregor, Ford. "The Municipal Reference Bureau." *NUEA Proceedings,* March 1915.

Melville, Andrew H. "The Field Work in Extension." *NUEA Proceedings,* March 1915.

Middlebrook, W. T. "Educational Sponsorship of Radio Programs." *Education on the Air.* Columbus: Ohio State University, 1930.

Miller, N. C. "Symposium on Teaching Radio Theory by Correspondence Instruction." *NUEA Proceedings,* April-May 1925, p. 128.

Monk, A. H. "Veterans Administration." *NUEA Proceedings,* vol. 35, April 1952.

Nash, Philip. "Cooperation with Other Institutions." *Association of Urban Universities Proceedings,* 1934.

Oxley, Howard W. "University Extension in CCC Camp Education." *NUEA Proceedings,* vol. 21, May 1936.

Paulu, Burton. "The Challenge of the 242 Channels." *NUEA Proceedings,* vol. 35, April 1952.

"Plan of Work." *University Extension Bulletin* no. 2, University of the State of New York, Albany, September 1892, pp. 55–67.

Poston, Richard W. "Report of the Chairman, Division of Community Development." *NUEA Proceedings,* 1958.

Price, Richard R. "Minnesota's University Weeks." *NUEA Proceedings,* March 1915, pp. 60–61.

Raybould, S. E. "University Extra-Mural Education in Great Britain." *Universities in Adult Education.* Paris: UNESCO, 1952.

Reber, Louis E. "Self-supporting and Contributory Fees in the University Extension Budget." *NUEA Proceedings,* April 1917, pp. 12–13.

Reber, Louis E. "The Scope of University Extension and Its Organization and Subdivisions." *NUEA Proceedings,* March 1915, p. 33.

"Report of Summer Schools." *Home Education Bulletin* no. 30, University of the State of New York, Albany, 1899.

Riley, B. C. "Some Problems of University State Stations." *NUEA Proceedings,* vol. 14, May 1929.

Robertson, C. B. "Types of University Extension Development and Present-day Tendencies in the Eastern States." *NUEA Proceedings,* vol. 72, April 1917.

Robinson, Stanley C.; Short, Carter; and Falls, J. D. "Conferences and Institutes." *NUEA Proceedings,* vol. 35, April 1952.

"Salient Features of Current Programs for Adults in Member Institutions." *Association of Urban Universities Proceedings,* 1933.

Scott, Almere. "Replies to Specific Inquiries and the Circulation of Traveling Package Libraries." *NUEA Proceedings,* 1915.

Scott, Elmer. "The Program of the American Association of Adult Education." *NUEA Proceedings,* vol. 14, May 1929.

Scroggs, J. W. "Seventh Session." *NUEA Proceedings,* vol. 10, April-May 1925.

Shockley, F. W. "Report of the Committee on Statistics and Research." *NUEA Proceedings,* vol. 20, May 1935.

Siegle, Peter E., and Whipple, James B. *New Directions in Programming for University Adult Education.* Center for the Study of Liberal Education for Adults, Chicago, 1957.

"Significant Features of Adult Classes." *Association of Urban Universities Proceedings.* November 1928.

"State Leadership." *University Extension Bulletin,* no. 1, University of the State of New York, Albany, 1891.

Stover, Charles B. "The Neighborhood Guild in New York." *Johns Hopkins University Studies in Historical and Political Science,* vol. 7, edited by Herbert Baxter Adams. Baltimore: Johns Hopkins University, 1889.

"Summer Schools." *Extension Bulletin* no. 25, University of the State of New York, Albany, 1898.

"Summer Schools, 1900." *Home Education Department Bulletin* no. 36, University of the State of New York, Albany, 1900.

Swift, Morrison I. *The Plan of a Social University*. Philadelphia: Social University Monographs, n.d.

Van Hise, Charles. "The University Extension Function in the Modern University." *NUEA Proceedings*, 1915.

Wilson, Lewis. "The Emergency College Program in New York State." *Association of Urban Universities Proceedings*, 1933.

Wilson, Louis. "Extension Work in the Southeast." *NUEA Proceedings*, April 1917, pp. 77–78.

Woods, Baldwin M., and Hammarberg, Helen V. "University Extension in the United States of America." *Universities in Adult Education*. Paris: UNESCO, 1952.

Wostrel, J. F. "Teaching Radio Theory—Class Instruction." *NUEA Proceedings*, 1925.

Zook, George F. "Standards of Evening Sessions in Colleges and Universities of the North Central Association." *Association of Urban Universities Proceedings*, 1928.

Periodicals

Adams, Herbert Baxter. "A Letter to the Springfield Republican." *Library Journal* 12 (November 1887): 512.

Angell, J. R. "The Junior College Movement in High Schools." *School Review* 23 (May 1915): 289–302.

Blauch, Lloyd E. "Higher Education and the Federal Government." *Higher Education* 13, no. 4 (December 1956): 53–59.

Boughton, Willis. "University Extension." *Arena* 4, no. 2 (September 1891): 452–58.

Bryce, Lloyd. "The Example of a Great Life." *North American Review* 150, no. 413 (April 1891): 410–22.

Buckley, J. M. "The Cooper Institute." *Chautauquan* 5 (April 1884): 398–99.

Butler, Nathaniel. "The University of Chicago and University Extension." *University Extension* 3 (February 1894): 244–47.

Butler, Nathaniel. "University Extension Class—Courses of the University of Chicago." *University Extension* 4 (December 1894): 171–78.

"Changes in the College Housing Program." Higher Education 13 (September 1956): 13–14.

"C.L.S.C. Graduates—The Class of 1885." *Chautauquan* 6 (February 1886): 304–8.

"The Correspondence University." *Harper's Weekly* 27 (October 27, 1883): 676.

Editor. *Nation* 49 (September 19, 1889): 232.

"Editorial." *School and College* 1 (February 1892): 108–9.

"Education of Korean Veterans." *Higher Education* 12 (January 1956): 82–83.

Eells, Walter C. "Adult Education in California Junior Colleges." *Junior College Journal* 5 (May 1935): 437–48.

"Extending University Extension." *Independent* 74 (May 15, 1913): 1104.

Farber, M. A. "State Will Open College Without a Campus in Fall." *New York Times,* July 9, 1971.

Flood, Theodore, "Editor's Outlook." *Chautauquan* 9 (October 1888): 52–54.

Fowler, Ruth, and Bucharest, David. "The Junior Evening College Student." *Junior College Journal* 10 (February 1940): 318–20.

Frazier, W. T. "Federal Surplus Property for Education." *Higher Education* 12 (January 1956): 81–82.

"GI's at Harvard. They Are the Best Students in the College's History." *Life,* July 1946, p. 217.

Goddard, Roy W. "Junior College Serves Community Needs." *Junior College Journal* 4 (March 1934): 308–11.

Hale, Edward Everett. "The Chautauqua Literary and Scientific Circle." *Century* 9 (November 1885): 147–50.

Hard, William. "A University in Public Life." *Outlook* 86 (July 1907): 659–67.

Harper, William Rainey. "The Founder of the Chautauqua Movement." *Outlook* 54 (September 26, 1896): 546–50.

Holmes, R. S. "The Chautauqua University." *Chautauquan* 5 (December 1884): 170–71.

Hull, Richard C. "First Educational TV Station Serves the Community." *Higher Education* 7 (April 1951): 180–81.

Klein, Ralph J. "The University of Maryland's Overseas Program." *Higher Education* 13 (April 1957): 154–56.

Larned, J. N. "An Experiment in University Extension." *Library Journal* 13 (March-April 1888): 75.

Larned, J. N. "To the Buffalo Courier." *Library Journal* 12 (November 1887): 513.

"Local Circles," *Chautauquan* 3 (December 1882): 163–64.

"Lowell Offering." *Atlantic Monthly* 67 (April 1891): 570–71.

"Maine to Try Taking College to Student." *New York Times,* August 13, 1971.

Marcel. "To the Editor of the Nation." *Nation* 49 (October 10, 1889): 290.

Metzler, David R. "Student Opinion on Adult Education." *Junior College Journal* 3 (April 1933): 3–6.

Morse, Bradford. "The Veteran and His Education." *Higher Education* 16 (March 1960): 347–50.

Nalder, F. F. "The Opportunity and Demand for University Extension." *School and Society* 6 (September 22, 1917): 344–49.

Orvis, Mary Burchard. "Wisconsin's Package Libraries." *Independent* 72 (August 22, 1912): 436–38.

"A Plea for Chautauqua." *Nation* 49 (October 31, 1889): 350.

"The Publisher's Desk." *Munsey's Magazine* 13 (April 1895): 103–4.

Reid, Loren. "Speech in the Maryland Overseas Program." *Quarterly Journal of Speech* 42 (December 1956): 379–85.

Robbins, C. L. "Small Junior Colleges and Adult Education." *Junior College Journal* 1 (June 1931): 555–59.

Steffens, Lincoln. "Sending a State to College." *American Magazine* 67 (February 1909): 361–64.

"The Summer Assemblies." *Chautauquan* 5 (July 1885): 603–6.

"The Twelfth Chautauqua Assembly." *Chautauquan* 6 (October 1885): 43–44.

Walsh, John. "The Open University: Breakthrough for Britain?" *Science* 174 (November 12, 1971): 675–78.

"What Has the American Society Accomplished?" *University Extension* 2 (December 1892): 161–70.

Zook, George F. "Junior Colleges and Adult Education." *Junior College Journal* 4 (March 1934): 279–80.

Zook, George F.; Kent, R. A.; and Ellis, A. Caswell. "Evening and Other Part-Time Education." *North Central Association Quarterly* 4 (September 1929): 237–42.

Index

Aberdeen Proving Ground, 144
Adams, Charles Kendall, 83
Adams, Herbert Baxter, 76; quoted, 54, 55, 57–58, 60
Adams, T. S., 82
Adult education: contemporary trends in, 166–69; decline of, after 1895, 76–78; and the Great Depression, 127; in the nineteenth century, 13–35; radio and, 122–27
Adult Education Association (AEA), 159, 168
Adult Education Movement in the United States (Knowles), xii
Adult Leadership, 159
Agassiz, Louis, 58
Agnell, J. R., 118
Agriculture, U.S. Department of, 94
American Association of Adult Education, 135, 159
American Journal of Education, 16
American Association of Junior Colleges, 120

American Radio and Research Corporation, 123
American Society for the Extension of University Teaching, 62, 66–68, 69–70
American Temperance University (Harriman, Tenn.), 32–33
Andrews Air Force Base, 144
Antioch College, 123; off-campus program, 163
Applied Sociology (Ward), 84
Apprentices' Library Association (New York City), 19
Association of College and University Broadcasting Stations, 125
Association of University Evening Colleges, xii, 106, 168
Association of Urban Evening Colleges, 134, 135
Association of Urban Universities, 113, 116, 135
Autobiography (La Follette), 92

Baltimore, university extension in, 59
Barnard, Henry, 20

Bemis, Edward W., 61, 62
Benjamin, Harold, quoted, 147–48
Birge, E. A., 83
Birkbeck, George, 18
Bittner, W. S., quoted, 108–9
Bolling Air Force Base, 144
Boston, public library movement
    in, 16
Bowdoin College, 74
Boyer, Chancellor, 164
Bradford, Pa., 43
Brown, J. Stanley, 118
Brown, Robert, quoted, 150–51
Brown University, 11
Buckeye Mower, 39
Buffalo, N.Y., extension
    courses in, 60–62
Buffalo Courier, 60
Bureau of Education, U.S., 30, 31
Butler, Nathaniel, quoted, 70

California: expansion of junior
    college system in, 119;
    university extension in, 97–99
Cambridge University (England),
    49–57
Canton, Oh., 62
Carey, James, 167, 168
Carnegie, Andrew, 16
Carnegie Corporation, 134, 162,
    164, 168
Carnegie Institute, 103
Center for Continuation Studies
    (University of Minnesota),
    147–49
Center for the Study of Liberal
    Education for Adults (CSLEA),
    159–60, 168
Century magazine, 15
Chaffu, Maurice, quoted, 151
Chautauqua Literary and
    Scientific Circle, 18, 29; history
    of the, 37–49; summer work
    at, 73
Chautauqua Movement

(Vincent), quoted, 47
Chautauquan magazine, 42
Chicago, extension teaching in,
    70–73
Cities, growth of U.S., 1–2
Citizen, 76
Civilian Conservation Corps
    (CCC), 128, 131
Civilian Works Administration
    (CWA), 131
Clark University Children's
    Institute, 103
Coffman, Lotus D., quoted, 147
Coit, Stanton, 68
College Housing Act (1950), 143
College of Charleston, 110
College of Liberal Arts
    (Chautauqua), 44–45
College of Special and
    Continuation Studies (University
    of Maryland), 144
Colleges and universities,
    nineteenth century U.S., 5–12
Columbia University, 11;
    extension program, 103
Commager, Henry Steel, quoted, 4
Commons, John R., 82
Community development, 156–59
Connecticut, 152
"Continental Classroom"
    program, 155
Continuing Education Report, 152
Conwell, Russell, 22
Cooper, James Fenimore, 3
Cooper, Peter, 25; quoted, 24
Cooper Union, formerly Cooper
    Institute (New York City),
    23–26
Cornell, Ezra, 9
Cornell University, 9, 10, 29, 75
Correspondence study, 26–35
Correspondence University, 28–29
Crane, Stephen, 3
Creese, James, 109
Crimi, James, quoted, 169

Cultural institutes, 21–26

Dartmouth College, 11; U.S.
    Supreme Court decision, 6
Darwin, Charles, quoted, 22
Denmark, folk high school in, 147
Department of Debating and
    Public Discussion (University
    of Wisconsin), 89–90
Deppe, Donald, quoted, 152–53
Devlin, Laurence E., quoted, 153
Dewey, Melvil, 62, 63
Dickinson, J. W., 45
Drexel Institute (Philadelphia), 26
Dyer, John, quoted, 114–15, 135

Education, democratization of, 6–7
Educational television, 153–56
Eells, Walter C., 118
Egbert, James, quoted, 103–4
Ehrenberger, Ray, 145
Eliot, Charles W., quoted, 12
Ely, Richard, 48, 58, 82
Empire State College (N.Y.),
    163–64
Engineering, Science, and
    Management War Training
    Program (ESMWT), 136
England: origin of mechanics'
    institutes in, 18; university
    extension in, 49–57
Evening college, 109–16
Everett, Edward, 22
Extension of University Teaching
    (Creese), quoted, 109

Fallows, Samuel, 29, 30
Farmers' institutes, 19–20
Farm Youth Institute, 149
Federal Communications
    Commission, 153
Federal Emergency Relief
    Administration (FERA), 128,
    131
Flexner, Abraham, 171

Flood, Theodore, quoted, 42–43
Folwell, W. W., 117
Ford Foundation, 164
Fort Meade, 144
Fort Wayne extension of
    Indiana University, 125
Foster, Thomas J., 34
Franklin, Benjamin, 14; and the
    public library, 15–16
Franklin, James, 14

Gale College, 33
Garland, Hamlin, 3
Germany: influence of, on U.S.
    universities, 7–8; origins of
    correspondence study in, 27
G. I. Bills, post World War II,
    140–44
Gilman, Daniel Coit, 11, 59
Goddard College adult program
    (Vermont), 162–63
Goldman, Freda H., 161
Goodspeed, T. W., quoted, 72
Goodwyn Institute (Memphis), 26
Graduate schools, expansion
    of, 11–12
Graham, Dean, quoted, 30
Grattan, C. Hartley, 13, 73;
    quoted, 77
Great Depression, and adult
    education, 127–35
Greeley, Horace, quoted, 7
*Green's Short History of the
    English People*, 41

Hammarberg, Helen V., quoted,
    76–77
Hannah, John A., quoted, 149
Harper, William Rainey, 37, 67,
    70, 117, 118
Harper Brothers publishers, 41
Hartford, Conn., teachers'
    institute (1839), 20
Harvard University, 11, 12, 74,
    143

Hatch Act (1887), 19
Hazard of New Fortunes
   (Howells), 3
Heidelberg, Germany, 145
Henderson, George, 67
Henderson, William, quoted,
   100–101
*History of Adult Education in
   Great Britain* (Kelly), 50
Holbrook, Josiah, quoted, 16–17
Hopkins, Harry, 128
Hoover, Herbert, 125
Howells, William Dean, 3
Howerth, Ira, quoted, 97–98
Hutchins, Frank A., 85
Hutchins, Robert M., 171
Hurlbut, Jesse, quoted, 40

Illinois Wesleyan University,
   29–30
Immigration, U.S., 2
Indiana State University, 60
Industrial Commission, 82
In Quest of Knowledge
   (Grattan), xii
International Correspondence
   Schools (Scranton, Pa.), 34
International Lesson System, 38
*Introduction to Political
   Economy* (Ely), 48
Iowa State College, 124
Irving, Washington, 3
Ivory Towers in the Market Place
   (Dyer), xii

*Johns Hopkins Studies in
   Historical and Political Science,*
   58
Johns Hopkins University, 11, 12,
   58–59, 155
Joliet Junior College (Ill.), 118
Junior College Journal, 120, 122
Junior colleges, 117–22
Junto, the (Philadelphia), 15

Kansas State Agricultural
   College, 20
KDKA (Pittsburgh), 122
Kellogg Center (Michigan State
   University), 149–50, 151
Kellogg Foundation, 149, 151,
   152, 168
Kelly, Thomas, quoted, 50, 56
Knowles, Malcolm S., 166;
   quoted, 107
Kolbe, Parke R., 112, 115;
   quoted, 110–11
Korean War veterans, 142

La Follette, Robert M., 81,
   83; quoted, 82
La Guardia, Fiorello, 136
Lake Chautauqua, N.Y., 39
Land grant colleges, 8–10
Langenscheidt, Gustav, 27
Larned, J. N., quoted, 60–61, 62
Lawrence Scientific School
   (Harvard), 11
Legler, Henry, 85, 86
Leonard, William Ellery, 82
Lewis, Philip, 155
Lexington, Mass., normal school
   (1839), 20
Libraries, founding of public,
   15–16
Library Company (Philadelphia),
   15
Library of Congress, 15
Life, quoted, 143
Lighty, W. H., 85, 87; quoted,
   123–24
Litchfield, Ann, quoted, 153
Liveright, A. A., 161; quoted, 172
London Society for the Extension
   of University Teaching, 55
Louisiana State University,
   overseas extension program, 144
Lowell, John, Jr., 21, 22
Lowell, John Amory, 22

Lowell Institute (Boston), 21–23, 26
Lyceum, the nineteenth century, 16–18
Lyell, Sir Charles, 22

MacAlister, James, 67
McCarthy, Charles, 82, 85, 86
McClure, Merle, quoted, 150
McKenzie, Dean, quoted, 120–21
Magazines, literary, 14–15
Maggie, A Girl of the Streets (Crane), 3
Maine, 152
Main Traveled Roads (Garland), 3
Mallory, Hervey F., 72
Mann, Horace, 4, 20
Marietta College, 123
Marsh, C. A., quoted, 131
Massachusetts, 152; Department of Education, 125; farmers' institute, 19; public education in, 4
Melville, Andrew, quoted, 90–91
Mercantile Library Association (New York City), 19
Merchants and Manufacturers' Association of Milwaukee, 87
Michigan Community Health Project, 149
Michigan State University, Kellogg Center, 149–51
Middlebrook, W. T., quoted, 126–27
Military extension programs, 144–46
Millbury Branch Number 1 of the American Lyceum, 17
Miller, Lewis, 38–39
Minnesota, extension programs in, 94–97
"Model Community Development Curriculum and Training

Center" (Mohawk Valley Community College), 165
Mohawk Valley Community College, 165
Morison, Samuel Eliot, quoted, 4
Morrill, Justin, 10
Morrill Land Grant acts (1862, 1890), 8–10, 65, 110
Morton, John R., 112, 168
Moulton, R. G., 67, 72
Municipal Reference Bureau: California, 98; Michigan, 100; Minnesota, 97; Wisconsin, 88
Munsey's magazine, 15

Nalder, F. F., 98; quoted, 99
Nash, Philip, quoted, 130–31
Nation, quoted, 47–48
National American Lyceum, 17–18, 20
National Association of Educational Broadcasters, 154
National Education Association Department of Adult Education, 159
National Home Reading Union (England), 40
National Summer School (Glen Falls, N.Y.), 74
National University Extension Association (NUEA), xii, 105, 106, 113, 125, 168, 169; Division of Community Development, 156–57
National Youth Administration, 133
Nebraska Sunday School Assembly Grounds, 46
Negroes, colleges for, 10
Neighborhood Guild (New York City), 68
New England, public education in, 4
New England Center, 151–52

New England Courant, 14
New Hampshire, 152
New Jersey, nonresident college
   in, 165
Newsletter (Boston), 14
Newspapers, 13–14
New York City: depression
   education programs, 130;
   nineteenth century public
   education, 4, 5
New York Herald, 14
New York State: emergency
   college centers, 130; support
   for university extension, 62–66;
   teachers' institutes, 20;
   Temporary Emergency Relief
   Administration, 130
New York Sun, 14
Ninth Corps Area of the CCC,
   132
North American Review, 14
North Carolina, extension program
   in, 101–2
North Central Association of
   Colleges and Universities, 30
Northern Illinois College, 31–32
*Northwestern Sunday School
   Quarterly*, 38
Nott, Eliphalet, 11

Office of Education, U.S., xii
Ohio State University, 75
Overseas extension programs,
   144–46
Oxford University (England),
   49–50, 54–55, 57
Oxley, Howard W., quoted, 132,
   133

Package library service
   (Wis.), 88
Pahlow, Edwin, 85
Peabody Institute (Baltimore),
   26, 59
Penikese Island, 58–59

Pennsylvania State College, 125
Pentagon, the, 144
Pepper, William, 67
Ph.D. degree requirements,
   31–33
Philadelphia, 5; neighborhood
   guild, 68–69; Society for the
   Extension of University
   Teaching, 67
Phillips, Wendell, 22
Pittsburgh, first Carnegie
   library in, 16
Platt, J. E., 46–47
Poston, Richard W., quoted, 156
Price, Richard, quoted, 95–96
Progressive Era, 79–80
Public education, nineteenth
   century U.S., 3–5
Public Works Administration, 145

Queens College, adult seminars,
   160

Radio, adult education and,
   122–27
Reber, Louis E., 86, 91;
   quoted, 105–6
Reform, era of, 79–80
Regents of the University of the
   State of New York, report on
   summer sessions, 75
Reid, Loren, quoted, 146
Rensselaer Polytechnic Institute,
   10
Residential conference centers,
   147–53
Rhode Island, 152; Department
   of Education, 102
Riley, B. C., quoted, 126
Robertson, C. B., quoted, 102–3
Roosevelt, Franklin D., 108, 128

St. Louis, Mo., 62
St. Louis University adult
   program, 161

Sarah Lawrence College, 160
Schoenfeld, Clarence A.,
    quoted, 139
School and College, quoted, 68
School of Language
    (Chautauqua), 45
School of Theology
    (Chautauqua), 44
"Science Review" program, 155
"Sending a State to College"
    (Steffins), 92
Servicemen's Readjustment Act
    (1944), 140
Shannon, Theodore J., quoted, 139
Sheffield Scientific School
    (Yale), 11
Sherwin, W. F., 47
Silliam, Benjamin, 22, 58
Simmons College, 160
Skidmore College, 163
Smith-Lever Act (1914), 93, 94
Social reform, 2–3
Society for the Promotion of
    Collegiate and Theological
    Education at the West, 6
Society to Encourage Studies
    at Home, 27, 40
State University of Iowa
    (Ames), 154
State University of New York, 63,
    102; Empire State College, 163
Steffins, Lincoln, 92
Steward, J. D., 46
Story of Chautauqua
    (Hurlbut), 40
Stuart, James, 50–52
Studies and Training Program in
    Continuing Education
    (University of Chicago), 152
Summer sessions, 73–78
Sunday School Journal, 38
Sunday School Union, 38, 39
"Sunrise Semester" program, 155
Surplus Property Act (1944), 142
Swift, Morrison, 68; quoted, 69

Syracuse University, 160

Tappan, Henry, 117; quoted, 8
Teachers' Institute, 20–21
Teachers' Retreat
    (Chautauqua), 45
Technical institutes, founding of,
    10–11
Television, educational, 153–56
Temple University extension
    program, 103
Tewksbury, Donald G., 6
Thomas, F. W., quoted, 120
Thomas A. Edison College, 165
Ticknor, Anne Eliot, 27–28, 40
Ticknor, George, 27
Toussant, Charles, 27
Truman, Harry, quoted, 140–41
Tufts College, 123
Tulane University, 123
Turner, Frederick Jackson, 58, 87

Union College (Schenectady), 11
U.S. Armed Forces Institute, 136
U.S. Military Academy (West
    Point), 10
University extension programs,
    49–73; spread of, 92–94; at
    Wisconsin, 81–92
University Extension, American
    Society journal, 67, 76
University Extension (Morton),
    112
University Extension Act of 1891
    (N.Y.), 65
University of Akron, 112–13
University of Bologna, 171
University of California, 60;
    extension, 97–99; overseas
    extension, 144
University of Chicago; extension
    program, 70–72; junior college,
    117–18; summer session, 74–75
University of Indiana, 123
University of Louisville, 110

University of Maine, adult
    education program 164–65
University of Maryland, overseas
    extension program, 144–46
University of Michigan, 8;
    community program, 157–58;
    extension, 100–101
University of Minnesota, 160;
    Center for Continuation Study,
    147–49; extension program,
    94–97; Group Correspondence
    Study Plan, 129
University of New Hampshire, 151
University of North Carolina,
    74, 100–102
University of Oklahoma, Bachelor
    of Liberal Studies Program, 162
University of Paris, 171
University of Pennsylvania, 11;
    extension, 103
University of Pittsburgh,
    extension, 103
University of Toledo, emergency
    schools, 130
University of West Virginia,
    Appalachian Center, 158
University of Wisconsin, 74, 75,
    124; CCC scholarships at,
    133–34; extension program,
    81–92, 104–5
University of Wooster (Oh.), 32
University programs for adults,
    special, 159–66
University weeks (Minn.), 95–97
Urban universities, 111–16

Van Hise, Charles, 83, 85–87;
    quoted, 84, 88, 89

Vermont, 152
Veterans Administration, 139, 140
VHF band (very high frequency),
    153
Vincent, George E., 96
Vincent, John Heyl, 37–48
Vista Volunteer Program, 165
Vocational institutes, nineteenth
    century, 18–21

Ward, Lester Frank, 84
Wayland, Francis, quoted, 7
Weston, S. Burns, 69
West Virginia Appalachian
    Center, 158
WGI (Medford, Mass.), 123
Wisconsin, An Experiment in
    Democracy (Howe), 92
Wisconsin Idea, the, 79–106, 167
Wisconsin Idea, The (McCarthy),
    92; quoted, 82–83
WOI-TV (Ames, Ia.), 154–55
Woods, Baldwin M., quoted,
    76–77
Worcester County Lyceum,
    (Mass.), 17
Works Progress Administration
    (WPA), 128
World War II, the universities
    and, 135–37

Yale Report of 1828, 6
Yale University, 11
YMCA War Prisoners' Aid, 136
Young, W. R., 136

Zook, George F., 116